SCOTUS 2025

AF098504

Howard Schweber
Editor

SCOTUS 2025

Major Decisions and Developments of the US Supreme Court

Editor
Howard Schweber
Madison, WI, USA

ISBN 978-3-032-10230-0   ISBN 978-3-032-10231-7   (eBook)
https://doi.org/10.1007/978-3-032-10231-7

© The Editor(s) (if applicable) and The Author(s), under exclusive license to Springer Nature Switzerland AG 2026

This work is subject to copyright. All rights are solely and exclusively licensed by the Publisher, whether the whole or part of the material is concerned, specifically the rights of translation, reprinting, reuse of illustrations, recitation, broadcasting, reproduction on microfilms or in any other physical way, and transmission or information storage and retrieval, electronic adaptation, computer software, or by similar or dissimilar methodology now known or hereafter developed.
The use of general descriptive names, registered names, trademarks, service marks, etc. in this publication does not imply, even in the absence of a specific statement, that such names are exempt from the relevant protective laws and regulations and therefore free for general use.
The publisher, the authors and the editors are safe to assume that the advice and information in this book are believed to be true and accurate at the date of publication. Neither the publisher nor the authors or the editors give a warranty, expressed or implied, with respect to the material contained herein or for any errors or omissions that may have been made. The publisher remains neutral with regard to jurisdictional claims in published maps and institutional affiliations.

This Palgrave Macmillan imprint is published by the registered company Springer Nature Switzerland AG.
The registered company address is: Gewerbestrasse 11, 6330 Cham, Switzerland

If disposing of this product, please recycle the paper.

Contents

1 Introduction: The 2024–2025 Term: A Tale of Two Courts (and Two Constitutions?)   1
Howard Schweber

2 American Constitutional Democracy in Crisis?   17
Mark A. Graber

3 *The Supreme Court, the Lower Federal Courts, and the Executive*: McMahon v. New York   29
Joshua D. Sarnoff

4 "The Shadow Docket"   39
Julie Novkov

5 *A.A.R.P. v. Trump*: The Uncertain Future of Presidential Power in Removal Cases   49
Jonathan Hafetz and David L. Sloss

6 *Trump v. CASA* (2025): Birthright Citizenship vs. Universal Injunctions   61
H. L. Pohlman

7   *Wilcox v. Trump*: The Death Rattle of the Independent
    Agency?   71
    Jonathan David Shaub

8   *Federal Communications Commission v. Consumer's
    Research*: Applying the Nondelegation Doctrine to
    Agency Discretion over Tax and Fee Obligations   81
    Bernard W. Bell

9   *Barnes v. Felix* on Excessive Force Claims Against Police   91
    Jasmine Farrier

10 *TikTok v. Garland*: The Supreme Court's Ongoing
    Struggle to Embrace the Impact of Technology
    Continues   101
    Mark Rush

11 *Oklahoma Statewide Charter School Board v. Drummond*:
    Religious Charter Schools at an Impasse   111
    Lauren Gilbert

12 *Mahmoud v. Taylor*: A New Standard for Religious
    Accommodation in Public Schools   121
    Carol Nackenoff

13 *Catholic Charities Bureau, Inc. v. Wisconsin*: A Blip
    on the Roberts Court's Path to Narrowing the
    Establishment Clause and Expanding Free Exercise   129
    George Thomas

14 *U.S. v. Skrmetti*: Rejecting a Challenge to Bans on
    Gender-Affirming Care Without Resolving Key
    Questions About the Rights of Transgender Individuals   139
    Susan Etta Keller

15 *Free Speech Coalition, Inc. v. Paxton*: Sexually
    Explicit Speech Online and Age Verification   149
    Eric T. Kasper

16 *Ames v. Ohio Dept. of Youth Services*: The White
    Man's Burden   159
    Ion Meyn

Notes on Contributors

Bernard W. Bell is Professor of Law, and Herbert Hannoch Scholar at Rutgers Law School. He specializes in Constitutional Law and Administrative Law. Bell's scholarly articles have appeared in numerous law journals, and he is a frequent blogger on the *Notice and Comment* blog hosted by the *Yale Journal on Regulation*. He is also currently a public member of the Administrative Conference of the United States. Bell holds a BA from Harvard College, majoring in Government, and a JD from Stanford Law School. He clerked for US Supreme Court Justice Byron R. White. He served as an Assistant United States Attorney and then Senior Litigation Counsel in the Civil Division of the United States Attorney's Office for the Southern District of New York before entering academia.

Jasmine Farrier is Professor of Political Science at the University of Louisville. She is the author of three books on US separation of powers development and public law, including *Passing the Buck: Congress, the Constitution, and Deficits* (Univ. Kentucky 2021), *Constitutional Dysfunction on Trial* (Cornell 2019), and *Congressional Amivalence: The Political Burdens of Constitutional Authority* (Univ. Kentucky 2010). She holds a PhD from the University of Texas at Austin.

Lauren Gilbert is an independent legal scholar. From 2002 to 2024, Gilbert was a Professor of Law at St. Thomas University School of Law in Miami Gardens, Florida, receiving tenure in 2009. She is a graduate of Harvard College and the University of Michigan Law School. She began her legal career in Washington, D.C., at Arnold & Porter, working primarily in the area of international trade law, before traveling to Central America on a Fulbright and later serving as an investigator for the UN Truth Commission on El Salvador. She was the first director of the Women & International Law Program at American University's Washington College of Law before moving to South Florida in 1998.

Mark A. Graber is the Regents Professor at the University of Maryland Carey School of Law. In 2023, he was honored to receive a Lifetime Achievement Award from the Law and Courts Section of the American Political Science Association. Despite what the first two sentences may lead you to believe, most of his current work is best described as history. He is the author of numerous articles and books, including *Punish Treason, Reward Loyalty: The forgotten Goals of Constitutional Reform After the Civil War* (Univ. Kansas 2025) and *Dred Scott and the Problem of Constitutional Evil* (Cambridge 2006).

Jonathan Hafetz is a professor at Seton Hall Law School. Hafetz is an expert on constitutional law, national security, human rights, and international criminal law. He is the author of several books: *Punishing Atrocities Through a Fair Trial: International Criminal Law from Nuremberg to the Age of Global Terrorism* (Cambridge 2018), and *Habeas Corpus After 9/11: Confronting America's New Global Detention System* (NYU 2011), which received the American Bar Association's Silver Gavel Award for Media and the Arts, Honorable Mention, and the American Society of Legal Writers, Scribes Silver Medal Award. He is also the editor of *Obama's Guantanamo: Stories from an Enduring Prison* (NYU 2016) and the co-editor (with Mark Denbeaux) of *The Guantanamo Lawyers: Inside a Prison Outside the Law* (NYU 2009). Prior to joining Seton Hall, he was a senior attorney at the American Civil Liberties Union, a litigation director at New York University's Brennan Center for Justice, and a John J. Gibbons Fellow in Public Interest and Constitutional Law at Gibbons, P.C. From 2017 to 2020, Hafetz was on leave from Seton Hall Law as a senior attorney at the ACLU's Center for Democracy.

Eric T. Kasper is Professor of Political Science at the University of Wisconsin-Eau Claire, where he also serves as the director of the Menard Center for Constitutional Studies. He holds a PhD in Political Science from the University of Wisconsin-Madison and a JD from the University of Wisconsin Law School. His teaching and research is mostly focused on the US Supreme Court and the US Constitution, particularly the First Amendment and the freedom of speech. Kasper has published 25 journal articles and book chapters, and he has authored or edited 9 books, including (with Troy A. Kozma), *The Supreme Court and the Philosopher: How John Stuart Mill Shaped U.S. Free Speech Protections* (Northern Ill. Univ. 2024).

Susan Etta Keller is Professor of Law at Western State College of Law in Irvine, California, where she also served for many years as Associate Dean for Academic Affairs. She is a graduate of Harvard Law School and Harvard/Radcliffe Colleges, with an MFA in Creative Writing from the University of California at Irvine. Her recent scholarship examines the ways that language in judicial opinions and legislation promote and enforce the gender binary.

NOTES ON CONTRIBUTORS xi

Ion Meyn is an associate professor at the University of Wisconsin Law School. Meyn teaches in the areas of civil and criminal procedure, civil rights, and race and the law. His scholarship examines how the criminal legal system constructs and maintains racial and class hierarchies. He serves as the reporter for the American Bar Association Diversion Standards and as co-chair of the ABA Criminal Justice Section's Academic Committee. Meyn clerked at the district court for Sixth Circuit Judge Bernice Donald. He also interned for California Supreme Court Justice Ming Chin.

Carol Nackenoff is Richter Professor Emerita of Political Science and senior research scholar at Swarthmore College. She is co-author (with Julie Novkov) of *American by Birth: Wong Kim Ark and the Battle for Citizenship* (Univ. Kansas 2021). She wrote *The Fictional Republic: Horatio Alger, Jr. and American Political Discourse* (Oxford 1994) and co-edited several books, including *Stating the Family: New Directions in American Politics* (Univ. Kansas 2020) and *Statebuilding from the Margins* (Penn 2014). She is currently examining the role that organized women played in pressing new definitions of public work on the American state during the long Progressive Era.

Julie Novkov is the Dean of the Rockefeller College of Public Affairs and Policy, a Collins Fellow, and Professor of Political Science and Women's, Gender, and Sexuality Studies at the University at Albany, SUNY. Her research and teaching address law, history, US political development, and subordinated identity. She is the author of several books and co-edited volumes, including the award-winning *Racial Union: Law, Intimacy, and the White State in Alabama 1865–1954* (Univ. Michigan 2021), *Constituting Workers, Protecting Women: Gender, Law and Labor in the Progressive Years* (Univ. Michigan 2001), and most recently, with Carol Nackenoff, *American by Birth: Wong Kim Ark and the Battle for Citizenship* (Univ. Kansas 2021). She chaired the Political Science Department from 2011 to 2017 and was President of the Western Political Science Association from 2016 to 2017. She served as a co-editor *American Political Science Review* from 2020 through 2024 and is now a co-editor of the Landmark Law Cases and American Society Series at the University Press of Kansas.

Harry Pohlman is Professor of Political Science and A. Lee Fritschler Professor of Public Policy at Dickinson College. Pohlman's teaching interests include American constitutional law, other law-related courses, and political and legal philosophy. Pohlman is the author of an undergraduate constitutional law textbook, *Terrorism and the Constitution: The Post-9/11* (Rowman and Littlefield 2008). He is also the author of *May It Amuse the Court: Editorial Cartoons of the Supreme Court and Constitution* (with Michael A. Kahn, Hill Street Press 2005) and three recent volumes in the second revised edition of Rowman and Littlefield's *Constitutional Debate in Action* series: *Civil Rights and Liberties* (2005), *Criminal Justice* (2005), and *Governmental Powers* (2004).

Mark Rush is the Waxberg Professor of Politics and Law and Director of the Center for International Education at Washington and Lee University. He has been with Washington and Lee since 1990. He holds a BA from Harvard and an MA and a PhD from Johns Hopkins. Prof. Rush's scholarly interests are diverse. He has written extensively on US politics, Constitutional Law in the United States and Canada, elections and democracy around the world, and global affairs. From 2010 to 2013, he served as Dean of the College of Arts and Sciences at the American University of Sharjah in the United Arab Emirates. His current scholarly work and interests include presidential powers over foreign affairs, separation of powers, international politics, judicial activism, elections and democratic reform, civic education, higher education and law, and law and technology. He serves on the board of directors of IES Abroad where he is also chair of the general conference. He also served on the academic advisory board of ISA.

Joshua Sarnoff is the Raymond P. Niro Professor of Intellectual Property Law at DePaul University College of Law. He was a consultant to the World Health Organization's COVID-19 Technology Access Pool from 2021 to 2023, has testified before the US Senate Judiciary Committee, Intellectual Property Subcommittee, and from 2014 to 2015 was a Thomas A. Edison Distinguished Scholar at the United States Patent and Trademark Office. He is a registered patent attorney and a private consultant, has been an expert witness and mediator in patent disputes, and has submitted numerous briefs amicus curiae in the US Supreme Court and US Court of Appeals for the Federal Circuit on a wide range of subjects. He is a member of the Advisory Board of the American Antitrust Institute. His research and teaching focus on the intersections of domestic and international intellectual property law, environmental law, health law, administrative and constitutional law, and antitrust law. Sarnoff is the editor of and a contributing author to the *Research Handbook on Intellectual Property and Climate* (Edward Elgar Publishing 2016).

Howard Schweber is Professor Emeritus of Political Science and an affiliate faculty member of the Law School at the University of Wisconsin-Madison. He holds a PhD from Cornell University and JD from the University of Washington. Schweber is the author or editor of eight books (including two prior volumes in this series) and more than forty articles and book chapters.

Jonathan Shaub is Norman and Carol Harned Associate Professor of Law and Public Policy at the University of Kentucky Rosenberg College of Law. Shaub's research focuses on the Constitution's separation of powers, executive privilege, presidential power, government accountability, transparency, and congressional oversight. He teaches courses in constitutional law, federal courts, and executive power. He has served as Senior Associate Counsel to the President with the White House Counsel's Office, as an Attorney-Adviser in the Office of Legal Counsel at the US Department of Justice. He has litigated cases in the US Supreme Court, US Court of Appeals for the Sixth Circuit, and Tennessee Supreme Court as Assistant Solicitor General for the State of Tennessee, and spent a year working on US Supreme Court cases and other appeals as a Bristow Fellow in the US Solicitor General's Office. Shaub earned his law degree from Northwestern Pritzker School of Law and his BA in Philosophy and Religious Studies from Vanderbilt University. After law school Shaub clerked for the Honorable Paul V. Niemeyer on the US Court of Appeals for the Fourth Circuit.

David Sloss is the John A. and Elizabeth H. Sutro Professor at Santa Clara University School of Law. Sloss' scholarship covers a broad range of areas, including international law, constitutional law, and international affairs. His scholarship is informed by a decade of experience in the federal government, where he helped draft and negotiate several major international treaties. Sloss recently published a book about how the US Supreme Court is subverting American democracy.

George Thomas is the Burnet C. Wohlford Professor of American Institutions at Claremont McKenna College. He is the author of several books including *The (Un)Written Constitution* (Oxford 2021) and *The Madisonian Constitution* (Johns Hopkins 2008). He holds degrees from the University of Utah and the University of Massachusetts at Amherst and previously taught at Williams College.

CHAPTER 1

Introduction: The 2024–2025 Term: A Tale of Two Courts (and Two Constitutions?)

Howard Schweber

The story of the 2024–2025 Supreme Court is the story of two very different Courts. One is what might be called the Normal Court, the institution that hears cases, issues decisions supported by opinions, and uses these decisions to develop constitutional and legal doctrines that evolve over time. This year's Normal Court was remarkable for its lack of activity. There were relatively few cases decided—50 cases scheduled for arguments producing 67 opinions—and none carried anything like the significance of blockbuster cases from recent terms. The pattern is surprising, as over the past few years the Roberts Court has established a reputation for big decisions in highly contentious cases, leading us to frame last term's presentation around the question of how "radical" a Court the 2023–2024 Roberts Court had been. This term there were no cases about abortions or guns, no major free speech cases, no substantive decisions that further develop the Roberts' Court's theories of federalism and separation of powers. There were three cases related to religious liberty, none of which announced any new principle, although one extended the principle of parental control over education and a tie outcome in a case about religious

H. Schweber (✉)
University of Wisconsin-Madison, Madison, WI, USA
e-mail: howard.schweber@wisc.edu

© The Author(s), under exclusive license to Springer Nature Switzerland AG 2026
H. Schweber (ed.), *SCOTUS 2025*,
https://doi.org/10.1007/978-3-032-10231-7_1

charter schools is certainly suggestive. There were cases that addressed issues of discrimination under federal statutes and equal protection issues, but none that departed from the long-term trend in the law toward treating all discrimination claims the same regardless of the race or gender of the claimant. And there was a case that adjusted the standard for evaluating police claims of perceived threats.

Several of these substantive or "normal" decisions were 9–0, others involved splits that did not follow the 6–3 pattern of conservatives versus liberals. An analysis of voting patterns suggests that the new "center" of the Court comprises Roberts, Kavanaugh, and Barrett (https://www.scotusblog.com/2025/07/how-2024-supreme-court-term-fits-into-history-of-roberts-court/). The outcomes of the 11 cases described in Chaps. 5, 6, 7, 8, 9, 10, 11, 12, 13, 14, 15, and 16 were ideologically varied in their outcomes and reasoning. Certainly the decision expanding parental rights for religious believers in *Mahmoud v Taylor* and the decision upholding a ban on gender-affirming care for minors in *United States v. Skrmetti* were politically and legally conservative; equally the decision limiting police invocations of perceived threats in *Barnes v Felix* and upholding a contribution scheme for the funding of rural broadband development in *FCC v Consumer Research* will please political liberals.

But then there was the other Court, the Emergency Court. It has always been the case that, in addition to hearing cases with briefs and arguments, the Court has entertained emergency petitions to stay or impose orders, injunctions, and other judicial remedies. These decisions are usually reached without argumentation or briefing or public discussion, with decisions taking the form of unsigned orders issues with little or no explanation. Stephen Vladeck characterizes this portion of the Court's work as "the shadow docket," and has document the way the Roberts Court has used its shadow docket cases more and more in recent years, sometimes to announce major new constitutional doctrines—again, without briefing, oral argument, or analysis—and almost always in ways that favor conservative positions.[1]

This year's Roberts Emergency Court has been all about Donald Trump's historically unprecedented challenges to the normal rule of law. No President since FDR and perhaps ever has engaged in a similar pattern of claiming that he is free to ignore federal laws of which he does not

---

[1] Steven Vladeck, *The Shadow Docket: How the Supreme Court Uses Stealth Rulings to Amass Power and Undermine the Republic*, (Basic Books 2024).

approve; using executive orders to defund or dissolve whole agencies; firing federal employees in contravention of statutory protections; openly ignoring long-standing Supreme Court precedent on the grounds that he expects the current Court to overrule those precedents; reviving statutes not used in decades or a century and applying them to assert powers far outside anything originally contemplated; using threats of lawsuits, revocation of clearances, and withholding of grant funds to pressure institutions of civil society—media, law firms, universities—to agree to actions he personally demands. Many of these are things that other Presidents have done. The argument that the President has an independent authority to determine what the law says is called "Departmentalism," and it has been part of discussions of American constitutionalism from the beginning. Nor is it unheard of for executive branch officials to defy court orders on occasion.[2] And the assertion of direct presidential control over all agencies and personnel in the Executive branch is the theory of the unitary executive that has become a standby of modern conservative jurisprudence.[3] But no previous administration has displayed these kinds of conduct the frequency, consistency, and the extremely sweeping executive orders that Trump has deployed.

Lower federal courts, confronted by this flood of extreme executive conduct, have responded in the way one would expect of normal courts: they have issues more than 200 orders and injunctions blocking actions by the administration. The administration's response has been a case study in defiance; outright refusal to comply, evasion, misrepresentation, hardball maneuvers to interfere with the judicial process such as moving litigants repeatedly so they could not be located, and of course appeals to the Roberts Emergency Court to have lower courts' orders stayed or overturned.

In ruling on these appeals the Emergency Roberts Court supported the Trump administration at nearly every turn on almost every procedural matter, and declined to rule on the underlying legal or constitutional issues involved. In an exception, the Court ruled unanimously that the Trump administration must comply with a federal judge's order to "facilitate" the release of a Venezuelan national mistakenly deported to El

---

[2] Nicholas R. Parillo, "The Endgame of Administrative Law: Governmental Disobedience and the Judicial Contempt Power," *Harvard Law* Review 131 (2018): 685–794.
[3] Stephen Calabresi, *The Unitary Executive: Presidential Power From Washington to Bush* (Yale University Press 2012)).

Salvador, though they remanded the case for the judge to clarify what "facilitate" required. In another case, the Court ruled that a minimum level of due process is required in deportation proceedings (see Chap. 5). But these were very much the exceptions that demonstrate the rule. The result of all the favorable rulings for the administration is that the Trump is free to continue in its actions that may eventually be found to have been illegal or unconstitutional, violations of basic rights, unauthorized, and potentially criminal were it not for the scope of the immunity granted last term by the Roberts Court in *Trump v. United States*.

These orders, issued in almost all cases unsigned and without explanation, were almost all decided 6–3. The dissenting justices' language has been unsparing, as in Justice Sotomayor's opinion dissenting from an order permitting the administration to proceed with dismantling the Dept. of Education, *McMahon v. State of New York*: "When the Executive publicly announces its intent to break the law, and then executes on that promise, it is the Judiciary's duty to check that lawlessness, not expedite it ... The majority is either willfully blind to the implications of its ruling or naive, but either way the threat to our Constitution's separation of powers is grave."[4] Will law students read that language in 20 years as a hysterical overreaction, or as a warning of dangers that are truly "grave"?

On a practical note, the *McMahon* case points to one of the difficulties in compiling this volume. It was necessary to select topics and recruit authors in the spring at the end of the normal Supreme Court term, but the Emergency Court has not stopped operating. *McMahon* is not specifically discussed in Chap. 5 for the simple reason that July 14 was too late for inclusion. And the emergency appeals and orders keep coming. *APHA v. NIH* application for stay of injunction July 24.[5] On July 31 the Federal Circuit Court of Appeals heard an appeal for repeal of an order of the Trade Court requiring Trump's tariffs to be rescinded pending an appeal of a ruling by that court that Trump has been acting illegally; a ruling is expected, and that ruling will certainly be immediately appealed to the Emergency Roberts Court.[6] Nor has Trump stopped asserting new, unprecedented powers. On August 7, 2025, President Trump signed an Executive Order that requires that all future grants for scientific research must, where applicable, demonstrably advance the President's policy

---

[4] *McMahon v. State of New York* No. 24A1203 (2025) (Sotomayor J., dissenting).
[5] https://www.supremecourt.gov/docket/docketfiles/html/public/25a103.html.
[6] *V.O.S. Selections, Inc. v. Trump* (Fed. Cir. Nos. 25-1812, 25-1813).

priorities" and "the national interest."⁷ Commentators recognized that what is going on is nothing short of an attempted transformation of the American constitutional system. As Lawrence Lessig frames the issue, There is no denying that the power of the presidency as Donald Trump is exercising it is far removed from anything any president before him has ever executed upon. He has in effect changed the nature of the presidency. Is that change for him alone? Or has Trump effectively amended the Constitution?"⁸

How should the Emergency Roberts Court have responded to the situation and to their dissenting colleagues? Many commentators have found the Court's actions—or inactions—to be deeply shocking, for at least three reasons. First, there is the apparent complete refusal to set any limits on the Trump administration's actions even where the underlying constitutional question seems to be crucially important, the harms potentially devastating, and the issues clear (the challenge to Trump's birthright citizenship order in *Trump v CASA* is a good example, see Chap. 6).

Second, the Roberts Emergency Court seems to entirely abandon any sense of solidarity with the lower federal courts; indeed, the relationship between the Supreme Court and the federal courts has been described as a "war" (see Chap. 3). Time and again lower court judges have found that the Trump administration has defied their orders, willfully violated the law, or acted in bad faith, and essentially every time, the Court has sided with Trump and slapped down the lower court judges. Dissenting in the birthright citizenship case, for example, Justice Ketanji Brown Jackson said, "In essence, the Court has now shoved lower court judges out of the way in cases where executive action is challenged, and has gifted the Executive with the prerogative of sometimes disregarding the law."⁹

Third, there is the apparent inconsistency in the way these matters have been treated since Trump took office in January 2025 compared with the way they were treated during the Biden administration (see Chap. 3). Mark Joseph Stern, discussing *McMahon*, points out the inconsistency. "The conservative justices, for instance, allowed a lower court to impose a universal injunction against Biden's student loan plan for months. It then

---

⁷ https://www.whitehouse.gov/presidential-actions/2025/08/improving-oversight-of-federal-grantmaking/

⁸ Laurence Lessig, "Could This Supreme Court Restrain Trump Even if it Wanted To?" https://slate.com/news-and-politics/2025/07/can-the-supreme-court-stop-donald-trump-history.html 7/22/25.

⁹ *CASA* 606 US ___ (2025) (Jackson, J., dissenting).

declared the plan unlawful, in part because mass debt relief was a 'major question' reserved to Congress. Now, not even six months into Trump's second term, these same justices have abolished universal injunctions and decided that the Education Department's termination is *not* a major question reserved to Congress. Could anyone really defend this partisan hypocrisy with a straight face?"[10] And dissenting justices have not failed to point out the apparently disregard for precedent and principle in some of the majority's positions. In August 2025 Justice Jackson reacted to a one-paragraph emergency ruling striking down a 106-page District Court ruling and order that would have required the restoration of funding awarded by the NIH while a challenge to the legality of those grant cancellations under the APA goes forward. Dissenting, Justice Jackson described the unexplained emergency order with a reference to popular culture. "'[R]ight when the Judiciary should be hunkering down to do all it can to preserve the law's constraints,' the Court opts instead to make vindicating the rule of law and preventing manifestly injurious Government action as difficult as possible. This is Calvinball jurisprudence with a twist. Calvinball has only one rule: There are no fixed rules. We seem to have two: that one, and this Administration always wins."[11]

The justices in the majority seem not to have been impressed by the expressions of outrage from either their dissenting colleagues or legal academics. Justice Kavanaugh defended the reliance on unexplained rulings in the shadow docket on the grounds that delaying reaching conclusions is actually a judicial virtue. "There can be a risk, in writing the opinion, of a lock-in effect, of making a snap judgment and putting it in writing, in a written opinion that's not going to reflect the final view."[12] Justice Alito describes the operation of the shadow docket as the equivalent of emergency medicine. "You can't expect the E.M.T.s and the emergency rooms to do the same thing that a team of physicians and nurses will do when

---

[10] Mark Joseph Stern, "The Supreme Court's Latest Gift to Trump is a Dark Turning Point," *Slate* July 15, 2025, https://slate.com/news-and-politics/2025/07/supreme-court-trump-department-of-education-disaster.html.

[11] *NIH v. American Public Health Ass'n.*, No. 25A103, 17 (2025)(Jackson, J., dissenting).

[12] Adam Liptak, "Kavanaugh Defends Supreme Court's Terse Emergency Orders," *New York Times* July 31, 2025. https://www.nytimes.com/2025/07/31/us/politics/kavanaugh-supreme-court-emergency.html.

they are handling a matter when time is not of the essence in the same way."[13]

The difficulty for an observer is that none of these justifications do anything to explain the extraordinary consistency with which the Trump administration wins in the issuance of these orders in ways and on legal bases that seem inconsistent with the adjudications going on in the Roberts Normal Court. Nor do the comments from Alito and Kavanaugh do anything to explain *why* the majority is unable to reach a conclusion on the underlying issues even in cases that strike nearly all observers as extreme. Justices Sotomayor, Kagan, and Jackson have accused the Roberts Emergency Court of deliberately intervening to permit lawlessness to run rampant. The response that prudence dictates inaction is difficult to credit as a legal, rather than a purely political, strategy.

One can imagine that in a year or two years we will look back and explain the apparent inconsistencies in one of the following three ways or some combination of them:

- The cynical political explanation suggested by Justice Jackson: The justices in the majority are either too intimidated by Trump to stand up to him or so supportive of his agenda that they will let it proceed even if they cannot find a way to describe his actions as either legal or constitutional. An even more (perhaps) cynical version of this explanation suggests that the justices in the majority will reverse course when and if there is a Democratic president at some point in the future. In this theory the reason the justices are refraining from making substantive rulings is that they will not have to explain their reversal of course when it happens.
- The "buying time" explanation: There are separate rules for right now as a temporary. matter. The reason the justices are refraining from making substantive rulings is that they are trying to delay, perhaps in the hope that many of these issues will go away after the midterms or the next presidential election and thus spare the Court the necessity of inserting itself into deep political conflicts.
- The legal revolution explanation: The justices are simply taking advantage of the chance to implement doctrinal principles that they

---

[13] Adam Liptak, ""Supreme Court Keeps Ruling in Trump's Favor, But it Doesn't Say Why," *New York Times* July 16, 2025 https://www.nytimes.com/2025/07/16/us/politics/supreme-courts-shadow-docket.html.

have wanted to enact, and the later substantive rulings will confirm the contours of the new constitutional order. This is arguably the explanation that makes the most sense of Justices Alito and Kavanaugh's explanation for the failure to issue substantive rulings right away: the details are still being worked out.

Many commentators have tended to focus on the second, institutional explanation. This exchange between William Baude and Steven Vladeck is illuminating:

> Baude: "[I]f we want to be more realistic about it, even if you wanted the court to maximally stop the Trump administration, surely it would need to pick and choose its spots carefully. There's just too much lawlessness to do otherwise."

> Vladeck: "That's a lesson for the court, too—that, insofar as some of its behavior this term can be explained as an effort to kick things down the road and avoid unnecessary confrontations with the executive branch, that bill is going to come due, and soon."[14]

All of which brings us back to the question with which this discussion started. We seem to have two distinct Courts; are they administering two different Constitutions?

Summary of Case Holdings

The one-sentence summaries and the table below provide a brief overview of the year's rulings that are explored in Chaps. 5, 6, 7, 8, 9, 10, 11, 12, 13, 14, 15, and 16, followed by a more detailed description of some of the dominant themes in those cases (Table 1.1).

---

[14] https://www.nytimes.com/2025/07/03/opinion/supreme-court-trump.html

Table 1.1 2023–2024 major cases

Ch	Case	Issue and outcome	Vote	Majority (author)
5	*J.G.G. v. Trump* and *A.A.R.P. v. Trump*	On habeas petition, due process required before the President uses the Enemy Aliens Act to deport undocumented immigrants without resolution of underlying question	5-4/7-2	*Per curiam/per curiam*
6	*Trump v. CASA*	On question of revocation of birthright citizenship, universal injunction struck down without resolution of underlying question	6-3	Barrett (6 conservatives); Kagan, Sotomayor, Jackson dissenting
7	*Wilcox v. Trump*	Stay issued to stop operation of injunction prohibiting President from dismissing agency head without resolution of underlying question	6-3	*Per curiam*, Kagan, Sotomayor, Jackson dissenting
8	*FCC v. Consumer Research*	FCC's universal service contribution scheme does not violate anti-delegation principles	6-3	Kagan; Gorsuch, Thomas, Alito dissenting
9	*Barnes v. Felix*	In evaluating reasonableness of officer's actions, "totality of circumstances" rather than "moment of threat" test applies	9-0	Kagan
10	*Tik Tok v. Garland*	Executive Order requiring ByteDance Co. to divest ownership of TikTok does not violate the First Amendment	9-0	*Per curiam*; Sotomayor, Gorsuch concurring
11	*Oklahoma Statewide Charter Comm'n. v. Drummond*	Grant of state charter to religious educational institution violates the Fourth Amendment	4-4	*Per curiam*, Justice Barrett not participating
12	*Mahmoud v. Taylor*	Parents have a constitutional right to excuse their children from school assignments that offend their religious beliefs	6-3	Alito; Sotomayor, Kagan, Jackson dissenting
13	*Catholic Charities Bureau, Inc. v. Wisc. Labor and Industry Comm'n.*	Hospital operated by Catholic Charities cannot be required to make contribution to state's unemployment compensation fund	9-0	Sotomayor, 9-0

(*continued*)

Table 1.1 (continued)

Ch	Case	Issue and outcome	Vote	Majority (author)
14	*United States v. Skrmetti*	Law banning gender-affirming care for minors does not violate the Fourteenth Amendment	6–3	Roberts; Sotomayor, Kagan, Jackson dissenting
15	*Free Speech Coalition v. Paxton*	Age verification system for access to online adult content subject to intermediate scrutiny, upheld	6–3	Thomas; Sotomayor, Kaga, Jackson dissenting
16	*Ames v. Ohio Dept. of Youth Services*	Under federal law, the test for discrimination based on gender is the same for a heterosexual or a non-heterosexual plaintiff	9–0	Jackson

Note: In the table above, **Issue** describes the broad topic at hand; **Vote** describes the majority and dissenting positions among the nine Justices; **Author (Majority)** notes the ideological grouping among the Justices. In general, the six conservative Justices are considered to be Samuel Alito (appointed by George W. Bush), Amy Coney Barrett (Trump), Neil Gorsuch (Trump), Brett Kavanaugh (Trump), Chief Justice John Roberts (George W. Bush), and Clarence Thomas (George H.W. Bush); the liberal Justices are Ketanji Brown Jackson (Biden), Elena Kagan (Obama), and Sonia Sotomayor (Obama)

CASES BY SUBJECT MATTER

President Trump (J.G.G. v. Trump, A.A.R.P. v. Trump, Trump v. Wilcox, Trump v. CASA)

These four cases were chosen for treatment because of the importance of the issues they raised: there were many other cases on the emergency docket involving challenges to Trump's exercise of authority in ways that were alleged to violate the Constitution or federal law (see Chap. 4). And there were other cases that could have been chosen, as well, involving the incredibly contentious relationship between Trump and the federal courts that features the administration's efforts to evade, ignore, and delay compliance with literally hundreds of judges' orders as well as appeals of some of those orders to the Supreme Court (see Chap. 3).

What all four of these cases—and many others—have in common was two things: first, that the Court sided with the Trump administration; and second, that the Court did so without ruling on the underlying issues in each case. All four cases are therefore ongoing.

J.G.G. v. Trump and *A.A.R.P. v. Trump* involve a challenge to the administration's attempt to deport people under the rarely invoked Enemy

Aliens Act of 1798. In both cases the Court ruled that the administration has to provide adequate procedures to allow individuals to challenge the basis of their deportation; neither case addressed the question of whether the eighteenth-century Enemy Aliens Act can be used to deport individuals on the theory that a criminal gang is *de facto* an agent of the Venezuelan government and that situation fits the scope of the statute.

Trump v. CASA is unusual in this group only because it features an actual written opinion containing legal reasoning. The case involves a challenge to Trump's Executive Order ending universal birthright citizenship. A lower court issued an injunction preventing the federal government from implementing that order, a so-called "universal injunction." The Court ruled that where private parties are concerned, lower courts cannot issue injunctions binding on the whole federal government. The majority opinion left open the possibility, however, that such injunctions may be justified where States are parties because of the administrative burdens that would be created by having different rules for citizenship operating in different States. The majority also suggested the possibility of using class action lawsuits that join together multiple plaintiffs as a way to reach federal operations across the country. Lower courts have followed the majority's lead: the 9th Circuit has ruled the Executive Order on birthright citizenship unconstitutional, and has ordered a universal injunction against the implementation of the order by virtue of the presence of States as parties,[15] and as of August 1 two District Courts have certified classes including all potentially affected persons so that the cases can go forward and issued injunctions against enforcement of the order; these rulings that are presently on appeal to the Fifth and Second Circuits, respectively.[16] There was no ruling on the underlying question of whether the President has the authority to change the understanding of the Constitution in the way that Trump is attempting.

Trump v. Wilcox is one of numerous cases involving challenges to Trump's efforts to dismiss civil servants who are protected by federal statute from dismissal except "for cause." The constitutional question is whether such for cause limitations on the President's dismissal authority are unconstitutional. This question was decided in favor of the

---

[15] *Washington v. Trump* 9th Cir No. 25-807, 7/28/25.
[16] *J.A.V. v. Trump*, No. 1:2025cv00072 (S.D. Texas 2025), on appeal to Fifth Circuit *W.M.M. et. Al. v. Trump*, No. 25-10534; *G.F.F. et al v. Trump*, No. 1:2025cv02886 (S.D.N.Y. 2025), on appeal to Second Circuit Court of Appeals No. 25-167.

constitutionality of such provisions in *Humphrey's Executor* in 1937; the Trump administration does not purport to be complying with that precedent or any of the federal laws enacted on its basis, they assert that the President is not bound to follow laws he finds to impose unconstitutional constraints on his authority, in this case under the theory of the unitary executive mentioned above. In *Wilcox* the Court issued an unsigned order permitting the administration to continue with challenged dismissals. Again, the Court did not address either the constitutional question or the legitimacy of a President ignoring existing precedents and laws the Court itself has ruled to be constitutionally legitimate.

*Religious Liberty (*Oklahoma Statewide Charter Comm'n. v. Drummond, Mahmoud v Taylor, Catholic Charities Bureau, Inc. v. Wis. Labor and Industry Review Comm'n*)*

All three of these cases concerned common themes, yet the range of outcomes across the cases is striking: *Drummond* was an inconclusive tie (4–4), *Mahmoud* reflected the ideological division among the justices (6–3), and in *Catholic Charities* the Court spoke in a united voice (9–0).

The charter school case raised the question of just how far the Roberts Court will go in its ongoing project of limiting the reach of the Establishment Clause. There was a time period when the idea of direct public funding for a religious educational institution would have been considered anathema; philosophically that "time period" can be said to begin with Madison's *Memorial and Remonstrance Against Religious Assessments* in 1785, but speaking legally the time period in question begins in 1947 with the Court's decision in *Everson v. Bd. Of Educ.* Is that principle still in effect? For the moment the answer is "yes," but only because of a tie vote in the Court as a result of one justice's recusal (Justice Barrett). The next time this issue arises, the outcome may be in favor of permitting the operation and funding of public religious schools; to say that would be a radical reimagining of Establishment Clause jurisprudence is an understatement. But that radical reimagining remains a matter for another term.

The second case, *Mahmoud v. Taylor*, involved parental rights combined with assertions of religious liberty, a combination that arises frequently in the educational context. This case can be thought of as the majority taking a principle that was designed to address a specific extreme case and applying it universally. The principle in question was that where continued participation in public education would threaten the survival of a prosperous (Amish) religious community, the state's interests are insufficient to justify compelling attendance beyond eighth grade. Or at least, that would be the narrow way of describing the ruling in *Yoder v. Wisconsin*. The version of the rule that emerges from *Mahmoud* is that any time a parent finds any educational content objectionable for religious reasons, public schools are obliged to excuse their children from exposure to that content. This is a classic clash between liberal and conservative cultural values, reflected in the 6–3 division in the votes.

The fact that the last case, *Catholic Charities*, was decided by a vote of 9–0 may be somewhat surprising. The question of whether religious believers have a right to be exempt from otherwise neutral laws that "burden" their religious practices has been at the forefront of Free Exercise jurisprudence since *Employment Division v. Smith* in 1990. In that case, Justice Scalia wrote an opinion saying that there is no such general right, but that states are free to create religious exemptions by statute. In the years that followed, courts—especially the Roberts Court—have limited the reach of the *Smith* principle by questioning the meaning of "neutral." Here, instead, the specific question had to do with the meaning of "religious"; the unanimous Court ruled that any time conduct is motivated by religious belief, it constitutes religious conduct subject to the protections afforded by state law. To fail to extent those statutory protections would violate the First Amendment because it would improperly distinguish among different religious practices.

Federal Agency Power (F.C.C. v. Consumer Research)

In the previous volume of this series, *SCOTUS 2024*, we wrote, "If there is one area in which the Roberts' Court's 2024 term is rightly described as "radical" it is this one," [referring to a series of decisions in the 2024 term that limited agency independence including *Loper Bright v. Raimando*[17] and *SEC v. Jarkesy*[18]]. This may not be surprising, as restructuring the system of federal regulatory agencies has been a core element of today's conservative judicial philosophy." In *FCC v. Consumer's Research*, however, the Court may be said to have taken a step back, or at least not gone further in the pursuit of restructuring executive agencies. The vote was 6–3,

---

[17] 603 U.S. 369 (2024).
[18] 603 U.S. __, No. 22-859 (2024).

with Roberts, Barrett, and Kavanaugh joining the liberals to uphold a contribution scheme by which the FCC funds rural broadcasting programs. On the other hand, the issue was not a core one unlike the issue in *Wilcox v. Trump*, and the theory that was asserted to challenge the contribution system, the non-delegation doctrine, was a reach. The Roberts Court has demonstrated it is sympathetic to the idea of non-delegation arguments, notably in its creation of the "major questions" doctrine. This particular application of the doctrine may simply have been too much of a stretch for the more moderate conservatives on the bench.

*Freedom of Speech (*Tik Tok v. Garland, Paxton v. Free Speech Alliance*)*

Neither of the two cases centering on the Free Speech clause looks like a classic example of the genre. *Tik Tok v Garland* held that Congress can pass a law requiring a foreign company to divest its US cyberspace operations under certain circumstances. That law poses a host of novel questions, starting with the very basic problem of using traditional First Amendment categories in the context of cyberspace. The fact that President Trump has repeatedly delayed implementation of the law on his own authority is yet another issue; that one may arise in a future term. The fact that the case was 9–0 reflects the shared recognition on the part of the justices that the complex swirl of issues involved—foreign trade, national security, cyberspace—made it a poor candidate for judicial intervention. Perhaps this might be greeted as a welcome instance of judicial modesty.

The other free speech case was *Paxton*. This case was much more traditional, and indeed raised issues that had been litigated in the past following the adoption of the 1996 Communications Decency Act. The real point of disagreement was theoretical; what level of judicial scrutiny is appropriate where a law burdens (but does not bar) adults' access to pornography in order to protect minors? The related question was whether the Texas law in question would really have its intended effect or whether the assessment of the burden on adults was being correctly evaluated. Disagreements on these rather traditional First Amendment questions account for the 6–3 outcome.

Equal Protection and Gender *(United States v. Skrmetti, Ames v. Ohio Dept. of Youth Services)*

Skrmetti involved a Tennessee law banning the provision of gender-affirming care to minors. The law specifically limited the medical treatments available to trans minors, an intersectional category that raises a question: for purposes of Equal Protection analysis should this law be understood as singling out trans people, or singling out minors? The majority said that the law was not aimed at anyone based on their gender, but rather was designed to limit medical procedures available to minors since trans adults could still get access to the treatments at issue. That framing—that the law is about protecting minors—meant that the State's burden of justification was very low. The dissenters, by contrast, argued that this was a law that *did* treat people differently based on their gender (cis minors versus trans minors). The background of the discussion is a Trump administration and a national Republican Party that is notably hostile toward trans individuals on the one hand, and different views in the worldwide medical community about the safety and efficacy of the treatments. The question therefore also involved the relationship between a court and experts and the question of who speaks for the American medical community. Chief Justice Roberts' opinion suggests a majority that is at a minimum not eager to address claims of discrimination on the basis of transgender status.

Ames involved a different issue of gender-based discrimination: whether in suits for discrimination under federal law the burden of proof is different for a cisgendered heterosexual plaintiff than for an LGBTQ+ plaintiff. The Court answered the question in a resounding "no," by a vote of 9–0. The case involved the interpretation of a statute, but the decision confirms the general intellectual move away from the protection of vulnerable minorities in favor of disfavoring all classifications based on gender equally.

Police Misconduct *(Barnes v. Felix)*

The ruling in *Barnes v Felix* was noteworthy in that it suggests that the Court may finally be willing to begin reining in the nearly unlimited latitude it has given to law enforcement in its qualified immunity decisions. The significance of the specific ruling for future cases is hard to predict with certainty, but at a minimum there is now a plausible basis for a plaintiff to ask a court to seriously consider the question of whether a police officer's use of forces is "reasonable" even in the face of that officer's assertion that he or she felt threatened at the time.

Conclusion: Two Courts (Two Constitutions?)

The answer to this deliberately provocative question is, no one knows. The next term looks to be truly extraordinary unless the justices in the majority decline yet again to answer the most important constitutional questions before it. Lower courts are continuing to declare the President's actions illegal or unconstitutional and issuing injunctions. Those injunctions will continue to come to the Supreme Court, and so will appeals from the rulings on the merits. Perhaps next term we will learn whether the Roberts Emergency Court has been signaling the appearance of a new and different Constitution from the one the Roberts Normal Court is used to.

CHAPTER 2

American Constitutional Democracy in Crisis?

Mark A. Graber

Much conventional wisdom proclaims the United States is experiencing a constitutional crisis. Members of the legal community declare the constitutional order is in crisis. A Westlaw search found 160 articles published from August 2024 to July 2025 using the phrase "constitutional crisis," most of which refer to the contemporary United States. Allison M. Whelan writes, "The United States is on the edge of a precipice, raising debates about whether the country is in a 'constitutional crisis'."[1] An article in the *Georgetown Law Journal Online* worries about the "potential for legal civil war" that "will come from a crisis in authority, the inability of mainstream institutions to retain sufficient legitimacy to govern and to counter the rising claims for authoritarian power."[2] The journalistic community is as

---

[1] Allison M. Whelan, "Foreword," 41 *Georgia State University Law Review* viii, xv (2025).
[2] June Carbone, Nancy Levit, and Naomi Cahn, "Legal Civil War," 113 *Georgetown Law Journal Online* 79, 96 (2025).

M. A. Graber (✉)
Carey School of Law, University of Maryland, Baltimore, MD, USA
e-mail: mgraber@law.umaryland.edu

© The Author(s), under exclusive license to Springer Nature Switzerland AG 2026
H. Schweber (ed.), *SCOTUS 2025*,
https://doi.org/10.1007/978-3-032-10231-7_2

concerned with the American constitutional order. The *New York Times* regularly refers to a "constitutional crisis." Headlines declare, "Trump's Actions Have Created a Constitutional Crisis, Scholars Say"[3] and "The Radical Legal Theories That Could Fuel a Constitutional Crisis."[4] Popular opinion agrees. The search engine of your choice will find numerous contemporary fears if you type in "constitutional crisis." The first page of my Microsoft Edge search turned up such gems as "LMV [League of Women Voters] Declares United States in a 'Constitutional Crisis,' Announces New Initiative to Mobilize Voters"[5] and a piece on the website of National Public Radio asking, "Are we in a constitutional crisis?"[6]

Constitutional law and constitutional pedagogy seem to be in a particular crisis. Over a decade ago, Professor Laurence Tribe abandoned his constitutional law treatise because Supreme Court decisions no longer had the coherence required by the treatise project.[7] Critics claim that incoherence has increased exponentially as the Roberts Court overrules or severely narrows precedents from earlier regimes, often on a "shadow docket," in which argument and deliberation are sparse.[8] Some professors are giving up teaching constitutional law while those who remain often find teaching emotionally wrenching. Jesse Wegman observes, "Even more troubling than the court's radical rulings, from a teacher's perspective, is the rapid and often unprincipled manner in which the justices reach them."[9]

Constitutional crises occur when the people of a regime experience severe difficulties operating the institutions of government and civil society to achieve constitutional goals.[10] Crucial segments of the population or political elite may be abandoning constitutional goals. Abraham Lincoln believed that Stephen Douglas and other mid-nineteenth-century

---

[3] February 10, 2025.

[4] February 15, 2025.

[5] https://www.lwv.org/newsroom/press-releases/lwv-declares-united-states-constitutional-crisis-announces-new-initiative

[6] https://www.npr.org/2025/02/11/1230674436/are-we-in-a-constitutional-crisis

[7] Laurence Tribe, "The Treatise Power," 8 *Green Bag* 2d 291, 292 (Spring 2005).

[8] See Stephen Vladeck, *The Shadow Docket: How the Supreme Court Uses Stealth Rulings to Amass Power and Undermine the Republic* (Basic Books: New York, 2023).

[9] Jesse Wegman, "The Crisis in Teaching Constitutional Law," *The New York Times*, February 26, 2024.

[10] For excellent typologies of constitutional crises, see Sanford Levinson and Jack M. Balkin, "Constitutional Crises," 157 *University of Pennsylvania Law Review* 707 (2009); Keith E. Whittington, "Yet Another Constitutional Crisis," 43 *William and Mary Law Review* 2093 (2002).

Democrats abandoned the constitutional commitment to place slavery on a "course of ultimate extinction."[11] Douglas accused Lincoln of abandoning the constitutional commitment to not interfering with slavery in states where that practice was legal. Constitutional institutions, when functioning normally, may not promote constitutional ends. A presidential election system that from 1788 to 1856 generated presidents with significant support in the free and slave states in 1860 generated a president supported only by free state votes.[12]

The most common form of constitutional crisis in many regimes is one of disobedience. Governing officials openly declare their intention not to follow the Constitution. Hitler announced his intention to overthrow the Weimar constitution. Autocratic leaders in other regimes engage in abusive constitutionalism, finding various means nominally within the constitution to change fundamental constitutional aspirations and purposes.[13] Such crises have not happened in the United States. Governing officials almost always declare their acts are constitutionally justified by the existing Constitution and express little desire to change the text fundamentally, if at all. President Donald Trump insists that all his actions follow from a constitution that grants remarkable powers to the chief executive. On the very rare occasions when presidents acknowledge they may be acting outside of the Constitution, Lincoln at the start of the Civil War which respect to a few of his actions and Thomas Jefferson privately with respect to the Louisiana Purchase, they insist that their unconstitutional conduct be constitutionally ratified after the fact.[14]

The constitutional crisis the United States seems to be experiencing may be taking two different forms. One form of constitutional crisis is

---

[11] Abraham Lincoln, "Mr Lincoln's Speech, First Joint Debate" *The Collected Works of Abraham Lincoln* (Vol. 1) (edited by Roy P. Basler) (Rutgers University Press: New Brunswick, NJ, 1953), pp. 18–21; Stephen Douglas, "Mr. Douglas's Speech, First Joint Debate" *The Collected Works of Abraham Lincoln* (Vol. 1) (edited by Roy P. Basler) (Rutgers University Press: New Brunswick, NJ, 1953), pp. 1–5.

[12] See Mark A. Graber, *Dred Scott and the Problem of Constitutional Evil* (Cambridge University Press: New York, 2006), pp. 159–67.

[13] See David Landau, "Abusive Constitutionalism," 47 *University of California Davis Law Review* 189 (2013).

[14] See Abraham Lincoln, "Special Section Message," *A Compilation of the Messages and Papers of the Presidents 1789–1897* (Vol. VI) (edited by James D. Richardson) (Government Printing Office: Washington, DC, 1897), pp. 24–25; National Constitution Center, "The Louisiana Purchase: Jefferson's constitutional gamble," The Louisiana Purchase: Jefferson's constitutional gamble | Constitution Center.

partisan. Major political parties and broad-based political movements dispute basic constitutional questions with each side insisting that their constitutional vision is the only legitimate understanding of the constitutional text. Each side insists the regime is experiencing a crisis of disobedience, since no fair person would regard the other side as making a good faith effort to follow the constitution. Unlike the crisis of disobedience, neither party to a partisan constitutional crisis acknowledges an intention even to change a comma in the Constitution. The Civil War was in part a consequence of this form a constitutional crisis. Both Lincoln and South Carolina claimed to be faithful to the Constitution, while insisting the other broke fundamental constitutional rules.[15] Another form of constitutional crisis is one of obedience. People are following constitutional rules to a reasonable degree, but those rules are not working as originally designed and wreaking havoc. The Civil War occurred because a presidential election system designed to ensure successful candidates had broad-based support in all sections of the country malfunctioned when unexpected northern population shifts enabled Republicans to elect a candidate who had no support in the slave states.[16] The flaw might be with constitutional institutions. Had the United States had a different system for elected the president in 1860, a candidate marginally acceptable to all sections of the country might have been elected. Alternatively, the flaw might be in civil society or the people. When people are as bitterly divided over some matter, such as Americans were in 1860 over slavery, no Constitution may be sufficient to hold the nation together.

---

[15] See Abraham Lincoln, "First Inaugural Address—Final Version," *The Collected Works of Abraham Lincoln* (Vol. 4) (edited by Roy P. Basler) (Rutgers University Press: New Brunswick, NJ, 1953), pp. 262–71; "Declaration of the Immediate Causes Which Induce and Justify the Secession of South Carolina from the Federal Union," *The Avalon Project*, Avalon Project - Confederate States of America - Declaration of the Immediate Causes Which Induce and Justify the Secession of South Carolina from the Federal Union.

[16] See Mark A. Graber, *Dred Scott and the Problem of Constitutional Evil* (Cambridge University Press: New York, 2006), pp. 159–67.

A Crisis of Partisanship?

Americans in the age of polarization are governed by two constitutions.[17] The Constitution of the Democratic Party does not limit government power to regulate the economy and guns but does significantly restrict government power to regulate sexuality and policing.

The Constitution of the Republican Party does not limit government power to regulate sexuality and policing but does significantly restrict government power to regulate the economy and guns. From the role of religion in public life to President Trump's use of executive powers, hardly any major constitutional issue in American life crosscuts the Democratic and Republican parties.

At the turn of the twenty-first century, the Supreme Court moderated the impact of political polarization on constitutional law. The two median justices on the Rehnquist Court, Justice Sandra O'Connor and Justice Anthony Kennedy, did not consistently side with either the most liberal or the most conservative justices on that bench. O'Connor often split the difference between rival factions. Her plurality opinion *Grutter v. Bollinger* (2003)[18] held that race conscious university admissions policies merited the strictest form of judicial scrutiny under the Fourteenth Amendment while sustaining race conscious admissions policies at the University of Michigan School of Law on analysis that seemed closer to intermediate scrutiny than strict scrutiny. Justices O'Connor, Kennedy, and David Souter authored the joint opinion in *Planned Parenthood of Southwest Pennsylvania v. Casey*[19] that reaffirmed a women's constitutional right to terminate a pregnancy while granting states far more power to regulate abortion. Kennedy often took positions on one partisan side or the other. He wrote the majority opinions in *Lawrence v. Texas* (2003)[20] and *Obergefell v. Hodges* (2015)[21] declaring constitutional rights to same sex intimacy and same sex marriage. Kennedy provided conservatives with a fifth vote in *Shelby County v. Holder* (2013)[22] when striking down a crucial

---

[17] H.W. Perry, Jr., and L.A. Powe, "The Political Battle for the Constitution," 21 *Constitutional Commentary* 641 (2004).
[18] 539 U.S. 306 (2003).
[19] 505 U.S. 833 (1992).
[20] 539 U.S. 558 (2003).
[21] 576 U.S. 644 (2015).
[22] 570 U.S. 529 (2013).

provision of the Voting Rights Act and in *Trump v. Hawaii* (2018)[23] when sustaining Trump's ban on persons traveling to the United States from many Muslim majority regimes. He was the crucial fifth vote in almost all cases where conservatives declared unconstitutional campaign finance regulations.[24] The result was the first court in American history to engage in judicial activism from the left and the right.[25]

Constitutional polarization has become more extreme in recent years. Moderate Republicans have all but disappeared as the Republican Party has moved radically to the right and Democrats more slowly to the left. The party in control of an electoral institution now runs that institution with little input from the other party. No swing justices exist on the Supreme Court. In almost every major Supreme Court decision, at least five conservatives vote against the three remaining liberals.

President Trump's policies and the progressive reaction highlight the structure of a partisan constitutional crisis. Trump in his first months in office announced constitutionally controversial policies by the day. These policies included deporting immigrants without hearings, challenging birthright citizenship, firing the heads of independent agencies, attacking major universities, impounding money allocated by Congress, using federal troops and state militia for law enforcement, abandoning long-standing environment programs aimed at combatting climate change, and gutting various departments to the point where their capacity to fill their mission was doubtful. Democrats and even remaining moderate Republicans insisted all these policies are unconstitutional. Crucially, for purposes of a partisan crisis, members of the Trump administration claimed each measure was constitutional. No member of the Trump administration insisted that Trump was violating the national constitution for the national good.

The Supreme Court now stands on one side of the partisan divide. Every Supreme Court decision that moves the needle moves the needle in a conservative direction. The justices favor Trump personally. Roberts Court majorities maintain that Trump and other presidents may not be criminally indicted for any act performed as part of him official duties[26]

---

[23] 585 U.S. 667 (2018).

[24] See, i.e., *Citizens United v. Federal Election Commission*, 558 U.S. 310 (2010).

[25] *See* Michael J. Klarman, "*Majoritarian Judicial Review: The Entrenchment Problem*," 85 *Georgetown Law Journal* 491, 548–49 (1997).

[26] *Trump v. United States*, 603 U.S. 593 (2024).

and that states have no power to disqualify him or other candidates for the presidency under Section Three of the Fourteenth Amendment.[27] The justices favor Trump administration policies. The Roberts Court insists that no constitutional right to an abortion exists,[28] but that courts should intervene whenever universities use race as an admissions criteria[29] or local officials regulate guns.[30] Religious claims are particularly successful in the contemporary Supreme Court. The justices maintain that a football coach has a constitutional right to pray in the middle of the field after the game is over[31] and that religious parents have a right to exemptions whenever they believe the school curriculum clashes with their faith.[32] The justices quickly intervene whenever lower federal courts attempt to halt administration policies.[33] Frequently, this requires use of the shadow docket, where the justices for all practical purposes decide cases on the merits without the benefit of extensive briefing or oral argument.[34] A cynic or political scientist might note that judicial minds tend to be made up on hot-button issues, so that briefing and oral argument would not likely be effective. Still, the extent to which the justices have abandoned pretenses of legality is another marker of a potential constitutional crisis.

The rhetoric of the Supreme Court has become more vituperative, even when compared to Justice Antonin Scalia's path-breaking trash-talking.[35] When overturning *Roe v. Wade*,[36] Justice Alito described the reasoning underlying judicial protection of abortion "egregiously wrong."[37] That word choice essentially described as incompetent his more liberal colleagues and a very high percentage of legal academics who insist the constitution does protect the right to terminate an abortion. More liberal justices give at least as much as they get. Justice Jackson, in particular, consistently accuses the justices of violating both constitutional and

---

[27] *Trump v. Anderson*, 601 U.S. 100 (2024).
[28] *Dobbs v. Jackson Women's Health Organization*, 597 U.S. 215, 231 (2022).
[29] *Students for Fair Admissions v. Harvard*, 600 U.S. 181 (2023).
[30] *New York State Rifle & Pistol Association v. Bruen*, 597 U.S. 1 (2022).
[31] *Kennedy v. Bremerton School District*, 597 U.S. 507 (2022).
[32] *Mahmoud v. Taylor*, 606 U.S. ___ (2025).
[33] See, i.e., *National Institutes of Health v. American Public Health Association*, 606 U.S. ___ (2025); *Trump v. Boyle*, 606 U.S. ___ (2025).
[34] See Vladeck, *The Shadow Docket*.
[35] See Sanford Levinson, "Trash Talk at the Supreme Court: Reflections on David Pozen's Constitutional Good Faith," 129 *Harvard Law Review Forum* 166 (2016).
[36] 410 U.S. 113 (1973).
[37] *Dobbs v. Jackson Women's Health Organization*, 597 U.S. 215, 231 (2022).

democratic norms. She described one decision as "not only truly unfortunate but also hubristic and senseless."[38] When the Supreme Court forbade lower federal court justices from issuing national injunctions, Jackson accused her colleagues of creating "a zone of lawlessness within which the executive has the prerogative to take or leave the law as it wishes."[39] Jackson described another decision as "Calvinball with a twist. Calvinball has only one rule: There are no fixed rules. We seem to have two; that one, and this Administration always wins."[40] "We will not dwell on Justice Jackson's argument," Justice Amy Coney Barnett snarkily responded to one of Justice Jackson's dissents, "which is at odds with more than two centuries worth of precedent, not to mention the Constitution itself."[41]

A Crisis of Obedience

Constitutional crises may occur, even when everyone agrees that the Constitution is being obeyed in relevant respects. Consider the claim that Trump's election initiated or aggravated a constitutional crisis. Trump's critics acknowledge that Trump in 2024 was elected consistently with the constitutional rules. He won the majority of Electoral College votes fair and square. Their objection is to the rules or the result of the rules. A different constitutional system for selecting or replacing presidents may have generated different and better presidents. Democrats might control the Senate had Americans never adopted or abandoned state equality in the Senate. Blind adherence to constitutional rules, in their opinion, is causing a crisis that would not occur if the Constitution had better rules.

The third decade of the twenty-first century is witnessing the most intense constitutional criticism since the Progressive era. Professor Sanford Levinson, a long-standing constitutional critic, identifies the following problems or "fault lines" in the Constitution:[42]

---

[38] *Trump v. American Federation of Government Employees*, 145 S. Ct. 2635, 2643 (Jackson, J., dissenting).

[39] *Trump v. CASA, Inc.*, 145 S. Ct. 2549, 2597 (Jackson, J., dissenting).

[40] *National Institutes of Health v. American Public Health Association*, 606 U.S. ___, ___ (2025) (Jackson, J., concurring and dissenting).

[41] *Trump v. CASA, Inc.*, at 2561.

[42] The following paragraph summarizes Sanford Levinson, *Our Undemocratic Constitution: Where the Constitution Goes Wrong (And How We the People Can Correct It)* (Oxford University Press: New York, 2006); Cynthia Levinson and Sanford Levinson, *Faulty Lines in*

- State Equality in the Senate
- The presidential veto
- The Electoral College
- The inadequate process for getting rid of presidents
- Life tenure for Supreme Court Justices

If this were not bad enough, Levinson points out that the undemocratic constitution is one of the hardest constitutions in the world to amend. Article V, he writes, is an "iron cage" that prevents Americans from responding to the institutional problems responsible for the present constitutional crisis.

The Constitution of the United States may suffer from two flaws. Some provisions may be inherently flawed. Democratic majoritarians strongly object to state equality in the Senate, the Electoral College, and other constitutional rules that enable popular minorities to control public policy. Other provisions in practice may generate bad outcomes. State equality in the Senate helps explain why such rural states as Wyoming get nearly the same amount of public transit funds per capita as such urban states as New York.[43] The Electoral College that was supposed to vet presidential candidates is now a formality.

Professor Maxwell Stearns focuses on the second of these problems.[44] He maintains that the Constitution creates structures that make good governance nearly impossible. The United States experiences either gridlock or presidential rule that some might describe as a constitutional dictatorship.[45] Stearns believes these problems might be remedied if the United States adopted three constitutional amendments:

1. Double the size of the House of Representatives and permit voters to cast one ballot for a candidate in a local election district and one for a national party.

---

the Constitution: The Framers, Their Fights, and the Flaws that Affect Us Today (Peachtree Publishers: Atlanta, GA, 2017).

[43] See Frances E. Lee and Bruce I. Oppenheimer, *Sizing Up the Senate: The Unequal Consequences of Equal Representation* (University of Chicago Press: Chicago, IL, 1999).

[44] This paragraph summarizes Maxwell L. Stearns, *Parliamentary America: The Least Radical Means of Radically Repairing Our Broken Democracy* (Johns Hopkins University Press: Baltimore, MD, 2024).

[45] See Clinton Rossiter, *Constitutional Dictatorship: Crisis Government in the Modern Democracies* (revised ed.) (Routledge: New York, 2002).

2. Parties select presidential candidates. The presidential candidate with a majority in the House becomes president. If no party has an absolute majority of seats, the party with the most seats gets to try to form a coalition (if that fails, the party with the second most seats tries to form a coalition, etc.).
3. The President may be removed for malfeasance by a vote of 60% of the House.

Stearns believes that because these amendments empower Congress, they are likely to pass the difficult threshold needed for constitutional amendment in the United States.

The problem of constitutional obedience may concern the fit between constitutional values, institutions, and people rather than simply flaws in the Constitution. Consider the consensus that the Constitution worked well throughout most of the twentieth century. The United States enjoyed unrivaled commercial prosperity and was seen as the model for other constitutional democracies. Lots of people had lots of quibbles, but few though their objections went to the American constitutional order. Today's sense of constitutional despair may be rooted in changes in civil society. The United States is a more diverse country than in the past, social media enables vicious lies and propaganda to be spread through the country, and racist sentiments some thought forever buried are reviving. The Constitution of 1787 is struggling to accommodate these political changes. Whether the American people of today can operate any democratic constitution is a fair question.

THE FUTURE

The good news may be that the United States is experiencing a constitutional crisis. Patients experience a health crisis when they need immediate medical intervention. Should that intervention be successful, the patient will be restored to good health. Terminally ill patients are not in crisis. They are going to die soon no matter what the remedy. The analogy to a medical crisis[46] implies that a successful outcome is possible if the remedy is applied in the very near future. Jack Balkin suspects efficacious remedies are nigh. He believes that American politics cycles between moments of polarization and depolarization, that the United States is merely in a

---

[46] Maxwell Stearns first pointed out the medical analogy to me.

period of constitutional crisis that will end as all other periods of polarization and constitutional crisis have ended.[47]

Others are less optimistic about the future of constitutional democracy in the United States. They worry that the crisis period has passed and constitutional democracy in the United States is now terminal. Garrett Graff, a prominent journalist, writes, "The United States, just months before its 250th birthday as the world's leading democracy, has tipped over the edge into authoritarianism and fascism."[48] Future editions of this volume, if permitted by future constitutional regimes, may document whether Balkin's optimism or Graff's pessimism is correct.

---

[47] Jack M. Balkin, *The Cycles of Constitutional Time* (Oxford University Press: New York, 2020).

[48] Garrett Graff, "America Tips Into Fascism," August 25, 2025, https://www.doomsday-scenario.co/p/america-tips-into-fascism-f51000e08e03254d.

CHAPTER 3

The Supreme Court, the Lower Federal Courts, and the Executive: McMahon v. New York

Joshua D. Sarnoff

Most of the executive branch of the US government is entirely a creation of Congress.[1] Similarly, the lower federal courts are entirely creations of Congress.[2] The federal courts police whether executive branch agencies have acted legally or illegally by interpreting statutes to assess the limits of agencies' legislatively delegated statutory authority. However, the Trump administration's relationship with lower federal courts has been more adversarial than any administration in recent history. In many recent cases, federal district and appellate courts have preliminarily found the executive branch to have acted beyond its authority, only to have the Supreme Court overturn the relief that those courts have granted. This is perhaps best illustrated by the recent lower court and Supreme Court decisions in *McMahon v. New York*, where various plaintiffs challenged the Trump

---

[1] See generally U.S. Const., art. II.
[2] See generally id., art. III.

J. D. Sarnoff (✉)
DePaul University College of Law, Chicago, IL, USA
e-mail: Jsarnoff@depaul.edu

© The Author(s), under exclusive license to Springer Nature Switzerland AG 2026
H. Schweber (ed.), *SCOTUS 2025*,
https://doi.org/10.1007/978-3-032-10231-7_3

administration's firing of almost half of the Department of Education (DOE) staff and the transfer of many DOE functions to other federal agencies. But first, some context.

Two of the key points of conflict that arise when determining legality of executive branch actions have to do with questions of judicial "deference," first to agency interpretations of their statutory authority and second to the reasonableness of an agency's policies or actions. The first is a question of legal meaning: the second a question of preventing arbitrary or unjustified administration. Federal courts must always determine whether they should accept (defer to) an executive agency's interpretation of the scope of its authority, or should determine those limits for themselves. Similarly, federal courts must always determine whether to defer to an agency's explanation of the basis for its policies or actions, or to independently determine whether the agency has adequately justified them.

The conflicts between the Trump administration and federal courts have all involved these questions of deference.[3] Unlike in the lower courts, many of the recent Supreme Court rulings evidence (albeit implicitly) a high degree of deference to agency interpretations of their statutory authority by overturning lower court orders that require the agencies in question to stop what they are doing. This is contrary to a major Supreme Court precedent from just last summer, when the Supreme Court restrained statutory interpretations of the Biden administration In *Loper-Bright Enterprises v. Raimondo*.[4] In that case, the Supreme Court eliminated the long-standing, so-called *Chevron*[5] deference to agency interpretations of their empowering statutes. "In an agency case as in any other, though, even if some judges might (or might not) consider the statute ambiguous, there is a best reading all the same—'the reading the court would have reached' if no agency were involved."[6] Given that decision, one might reasonably have expected the Supreme Court to encourage lower courts to adopt a skeptical attitude toward executive branch interpretations of statutes.

---

[3] *See, e.g.*, Sarah Paoletti, *Access to Justice, Deferred and Denied*, The Regulatory Review (July 29, 2025), at https://www.theregreview.org/2025/07/29/paoletti-access-to-justice-deferred-and-denied/ (discussing recent immigration cases and noting they represent "heightened deference to executive authority.").
[4] 603 U.S. 369 (2024).
[5] Chevron U.S.A. Inc. v. Natural Resources Defense Council, Inc., 467 U.S. 837 (1984).
[6] *Loper Bright*, 603 U.S. at 400.

But what a difference a change in executive administration can make. One would clearly have been wrong to think that the Supreme Court would be just as hostile to the second Trump administration's legal interpretations as it was to those of the Biden administration. This is true even though the *lower* federal courts (including many Trump appointees) now appear to be increasingly hostile to executive branch interpretations,[7] at least partly in response to the apparent lawlessness of the Trump administration.[8]

Others in this volume will focus on the Supreme Court's use of the shadow docket to stay or to reverse lower court preliminary injunctions that prohibited the Trump administration's ongoing illegal actions while litigation is pending.[9] Similarly, others will address the Court's restriction on the use of nationwide injunctive relief to prevent such lawless actions, except (where applicable) by class actions or where necessary to provide complete relief to the plaintiffs.[10] But I will focus more specifically how the Court has *implicitly* accepted the Trump administration's legal interpretations, by allowing agency actions to remain in place without deciding their merits. These Supreme Court decisions require lower courts to defer to the administration's interpretations and justifications, even when those lower courts have already found the challenged actions likely to be illegal.

Further, although the Supreme Court has indicated that lower courts are supposed to defer strongly to agency policy determinations and

---

[7] *See, e.g.*, Robin K. Craig, *The Impact of* Loper Bright v. Raimondo: *An Empirical Review of the First Six Months*, 109 Minn. L. Rev. 2671, 2732 (2025) (discussing the limited evidence to date, showing that agency rules fare worse than agency adjudications under *Loper Bright*).

[8] The lawlessness is apparent from the numerous preliminary injunctions, which require a showing that the action is more likely than not unauthorized by law. *See, e.g.*, Winter v. Nat. Res. Defense Council, Inc., 555 U.S. 7, 20 (2008) ("A plaintiff seeking a preliminary injunction must establish that he is likely to succeed on the merits, that he is likely to suffer irreparable harm in the absence of preliminary relief, that the balance of equities tips in his favor, and that an injunction is in the public interest").

[9] *See* Chap. 4. *See also* Stephen Vladeck, Bonus 170: Whose Judicial Overreach?, OneFirst blog, https://www.stevevladeck.com/p/bonus-170-a-reply-to-professor-adler (July 31, 2025) ("[A]t least *some* of the Court's behavior in these cases has in fact been *in*defensible—on procedural grounds; on substantive grounds; and no less importantly, on institutional grounds.").

[10] *See* Chap. 6, Trump v. Casa, 606 U.S. 831, 849–50 (2025).

justifications,[11] the Court appears to be deferring even more strongly for Trump administration actions in Administrative Procedure Act (APA) "arbitrary and capricious" review[12] than for actions taken by prior administrations.[13] Of course, this analysis is preliminary. It is possible that the Court will become less deferential to the Trump administration over time, given its persistent lawlessness, or when the Court actually reaches the merits of the Trump administration's actions. But by then it may be too late to undo the effects of the challenged actions. By staying the lower court's injunctions, the Supreme Court in many cases has effectively rendered any remedy in any subsequent ruling that the administration's actions were in fact illegal *practically* illusory to the parties and to the public.

In *McMahon v. New York*,[14] the Supreme Court without any explanation stayed a preliminary injunction issued by the District Court of Massachusetts,[15] which the First Circuit Court of Appeals had twice refused to stay.[16] The District Court had ordered reinstatement of DOE employees who had been dismissed by the Trump administration and had ordered restoration of DOE offices that had been disbanded.[17] The District Court preliminarily held that those actions were likely *ultra vires* (beyond statutory authority) and contrary to law (as specifically prohibited by statute), and also were likely arbitrary and capricious.[18] The DOE

---

[11] *See, e.g.*, Ohio v. Envt'l. Protection Agency, 603 U.S. 279, 292 (2024) ("a court may not 'substitute its judgment for that of the agency'") (quoting Federal Comm'n Comm. v. Fox Television Stations, Inc., 556 U.S. 502, 513 (2009)).

[12] 5 U.S.C. § 706(2)(A) ("The reviewing court shall—(2) hold unlawful and set aside agency action, findings, and conclusions found to be—(A) arbitrary, capricious, an abuse of discretion, or otherwise not in accordance with law").

[13] The APA is a "superstatute" that prohibits arbitrary and capricious action across all government agencies. *Cf.* Craig, supra note 7, at 2747 ("In the next few years, categories of agency expertise are likely to emerge, and the distinction between arbitrary and capricious review and statutory interpretation may become critical to whether individual agency regulatory decisions survive judicial review in certain federal courts.").

[14] 606 U.S. __, 145 S.Ct. 2643 (2025).

[15] New York v. McMahon, 748 F. Supp. 3d 311, 374, (D. Mass. 2025).

[16] New York v. McMahon, No. 25-1495, 2025 WL 1503501, at *1 (1st Cir. May 27, 2025); Somerville Public Schools v. McMahon, 139 F.4th 63, 67 (1st Cir. 2025).

[17] 784 F. Supp. 3d at 374.

[18] *Id.* at 352, 356–61.

actions followed a Presidential Executive Order[19] and Directive,[20] which the preliminary injunction also prohibited from being carried out or reinstated under a different name,[21] and had resulted in a reduction in force (RIF) "that impacted approximately half of [DOE's] employees" and that "transfer[red] ... certain functions out of the Department."[22] As the District Court noted, "President Trump has made his intention to dismantle the [DOE] publicly well-known, referring to the Department as a 'a big con job' and saying he would 'like to close it immediately'."[23] And as the District Court also noted, "Defendants argue that the RIF was implemented to improve 'efficiency' and 'accountability' in the Department. The record abundantly reveals that Defendants' true intention is to effectively dismantle the Department without an authorizing statute."[24]

In regard to statutory interpretation, the District Court made short work of the Trump administration arguments. The actions were likely *ultra vires*, because:

> As *Amici* Members of Congress explain, "no statute grants the Executive the authority to dismantle the Department because Congress has passed no statute that expressly authorizes the Executive to dissolve the Department or transfer its congressionally mandated responsibilities to other agencies."[25]

---

[19] Exec. Order No. 14,242, 90 Fed. Reg. 13679 (Mar. 20, 2025) ("(a) The Secretary of Education shall, to the maximum extent appropriate and permitted by law, take all necessary steps to facilitate the closure of the Department of Education and return authority over education to the States and local communities while ensuring the effective and uninterrupted delivery of services, programs, and benefits on which Americans rely."). Note that because the Executive Order is limited to what is permitted by law, it does not on its face *require nor authorize* any actions that are not so permitted, thereby (in theory, if not in practice) avoiding any direct constitutional conflict.

[20] *See New York*, 784F. Supp. 3d at 323 ("On March 21, 2025, President Trump further announced that the federal student loan portfolio as well as the special needs programs would be transferred out of the Department.").

[21] *Id.* at 374.

[22] *Somerville Public Schools*, 139 F.4th at 67.

[23] *New York*, 784F. Supp. 3d at 333.

[24] *Id.* at 323.

[25] *Id.* at 352–53 (internal quotation marks omitted).

Further, the District Court noted that "[t]he simple proposition that the President may not, *without Congress*, fundamentally reorganize the federal agencies is not controversial."[26]

In regard to statutory prohibition, the District Court apparently provided no deference to the agency, concisely dismissing the administration's arguments and interpretations.

> First, Defendants have not pointed to any case that indicates that the Secretary's effective dismantling of the Department is within her reorganization powers under [20 U.S.C.] § 3473 ... [T]o the extent that the Agency Defendants' actions are an effective dismantling of the Department, I find that those actions are contrary to the DEOA's mandate that the Department itself must exist—not just in name only, but to carry out the functions outlined in the DEOA and other relevant operating federal statutes."[27]

Similarly, but more narrowly, another district court preliminarily enjoined the reduction in force, holding that it adversely affected the ability of the Education Department's Office of Civil Rights (OCR) to perform its statutory duties and to "promptly" respond to complaints. Finally, in regard to the APA's requirements of reasoned (non-arbitrary) decision-making, the District Court found the articulated justifications entirely lacking.

> None of these statements amount to a reasoned explanation, let alone an explanation at all. Indeed, the March 11 Directive contains two contradictory positions. It states that the goal of the RIF is to improve the Department's "efficiency" but also states that the RIF has been taken to further the Department's "final mission"—which is, incontrovertibly, its closure.... There is no indication ... how any of those decisions further Defendants' purported goals of efficiency or effectiveness of the Department.[28]

Accordingly, the District Court found the actions taken to be arbitrary and capricious, and to prevent irreparable harm refused to remand for a further explanation (particularly as it had also found the action contrary to law, so no explanation could justify the action).[29]

---

[26] *Id.* at 353 (internal quotation marks and citation omitted).
[27] *Id.* at 359–60.
[28] *Id.* at 357–58.
[29] *See id.* at 357–60.

On appeal, after dismissing arguments based on lack of standing of the plaintiffs and other jurisdictional bar challenges,[30] the First Circuit dismissed the administration's statutory and APA arguments as not making the required "strong showing" of likely success on the merits.

> [T]he appellants do not even attempt to engage with the District Court's record-based findings about the extent of the RIF or the intent behind both it and the transfer of functions to shut down the Department. Nor do the appellants in making that assertion acknowledge, let alone meaningfully dispute, the District Court's record-based findings about the disabling impact of those actions on the Department's ability to carry out statutorily assigned functions. Rather, the assertion merely favorably characterizes the actions found to have been contrary to law and arbitrary and capricious as run-of-the-mill personnel decisions.[31]

Accordingly, the First Circuit denied the stay, emphasizing that "there is generally no public interest in the perpetuation of unlawful agency action."[32]

On further appeal to the Supreme Court, the six "conservative" Justices stayed the injunction without any explanation.[33] The three "liberal" Justices thought the case important enough to dissent. They noted the very high stakes involved, and first reaffirmed the constitutional holdings of the District Court that the Trump administration's actions violate the executive branch's constitutional duties, in terms that implicitly and harshly criticize their brethren for violating their constitutional duties.

> When the Executive publicly announces its intent to break the law, and then executes on that promise, *it is the Judiciary's duty to check that lawlessness, not expedite it.* Two lower courts rose to the occasion, preliminarily enjoining the mass firings while the litigation remains ongoing. Rather than maintain the status quo, however, this Court now intervenes, lifting the injunction and permitting the Government to proceed with dismantling the Department. *That decision is indefensible.* It hands the Executive the power to repeal statutes by firing all those necessary to carry them out. *The majority is either willfully blind to the implications of its ruling or naive,* but either

---

[30] *See Somerville Public Schools*, 139 F.4th at 68–72.
[31] *Id*. at 72.
[32] *Id*. at 76 (citation omitted).
[33] *McMahon*, 606 U.S. at ___, 145 S.Ct. at 2643.

> way *the threat to our Constitution's separation of powers is grave*. Unable to join in *this misuse of our emergency docket*, I respectfully dissent.
>
> ...
>
> The President thus lacks unilateral authority to close a Cabinet-level agency. Congress created the Department, and only Congress can abolish it. The President, too, may not refuse to carry out statutorily mandated functions assigned to the Department, for he must "take Care that the Laws be faithfully executed."...
>
> Rather than contest these bedrock principles, the Government below contended that the mass terminations were not part of any planned closure, but instead simply intended to "cut bureaucratic bloat."... The record unambiguously refutes that account.[34]

In judicial speak, that means that the government was lying to the courts.

Of greater relevance here, the liberal Justices (like the judges below) thought the actions were both *ultra vires* and prohibited by the relevant statutes.

> The Secretary, moreover, unquestionably exceeded Congress's statutory limits on her authority to reorganize the Department. Congress has barred the Secretary from "alter[ing]" functions assigned to the Department by its organic statute and from "abolish[ing] organizational entities" established by law.... The Secretary's failure to preserve statutorily mandated functions ... contravened that statutory constraint.[35]

Finally, the liberal Justices dismissed the "grab bag of jurisdictional and remedial arguments [asserted] to support its bid for emergency relief,"[36] and held that the equities clearly favored denying emergency relief.[37]

To the extent that the Supreme Court's conservative majority is implicitly announcing previously unknown legal principles, stays of lower court decisions without any articulated reasoning are certainly the worst

---

[34] *Id.* at 2644, 2649 (emphasis added and citations omitted).
[35] *Id.* at __, 145 S.Ct. at 2650 (citations omitted).
[36] *Id.* at __, 145 S.Ct. at 2651. *See id.* at __, 145 S.Ct. at 2651–53.
[37] *See id.* at __, 145 S.Ct. at 2653 ("The Government has continued to press a plainly pretextual explanation for the mass firings in court, even as the Executive makes inconsistent statements to the public.... That the majority sees fit to repay that obfuscation with emergency equitable relief is troubling.") (citation omitted).

possible way to do it.[38] And without such implicit changes in long-standing legal principles, the Court's ruling seems impossible to justify; the equities would clearly compel preserving the injunction.[39] Even if the DOE's actions were somehow found not to be arbitrary and capricious, absent new constitutional executive powers or new statutory interpretation or jurisdictional or remedial principles, the challenged actions would remain *ultra vires* and contrary to statute.

We don't actually know the Supreme Court majority's thinking. But none of the lower courts even attempted to analyze whether the President had independent authority to disband the DOE and fire half of its employees. Again, the District Court expressly stated that the lack of such authority was not controversial (meaning not *reasonably* disputable). Thus, this case is not (to date) a direct conflict between the President and the Congress. Rather, it is a proxy war, with the President encouraging the *agency* to disobey Congress. It thus remains (like many of the pending disputes) a judicial question of deference to agency interpretations and actions, and not an issue of constitutional powers of the President nor of any purported need for the President to exercise unilateral control over a "unitary executive." We will only learn otherwise if the case reaches the Court on the merits.

Without such newly found inherent executive powers or interpretive principles broading the scope of existing delegated authorities, moreover, by the time any merits decision could be reached by the Court that holds the DOE's actions to be illegal, most of the employees likely will have moved on or may refuse reinstatement. The public also will have incurred numerous harms (including schools and businesses shutting down) from DOE's failure to provide the statutorily contemplated grants and services. This is not normal judicial process, but the likely intended consequence of the Supreme Court's exercise of judicial power. Small wonder the liberal dissenters were harsh with their colleagues. We can expect many more

---

[38] *See, e.g.*, Kim Lane Scheppele, Chautauqua Institution Robert H. Jackson Lecture (Aug. 11, 2025), at https://www.youtube.com/watch?v=JXwQYL8d6kc ("We don't know what the law is. The Supreme Court changes its mind every day, with no warning and no reasons.... This is really lawless behavior and that's why this is dangerous.").

[39] Even where compelled reinstatement of illegally dismissed personnel somehow beyond administrative or judicial power, the First Circuit rejected arguments that such a limitation would prevent courts from prohibiting an unauthorized reorganization or massive dismissals that preclude the agency from carrying out its statutory functions. *See Somerville Public Schools*, 139 F.4th at 73–74.

such conflicts, so long as the conservative majority continues to defer implicitly or explicitly to the Trump administration's lawless statutory interpretations and arbitrary policies, or articulates new executive powers and interpretive principles, on both the emergency and regular merits dockets.

CHAPTER 4

"The Shadow Docket"

Julie Novkov

When we discuss the Court's major rulings in any given year, we generally talk about its rulings on the merits—rulings that usually follow a choreography of selection by the Court through *certiorari*, briefings, oral arguments, drafting and polishing of opinions, and then release of these rulings in a public session of the Court on designated weekday mornings.[1] But a lot of the Court's work does not proceed this way. The Justices dispose of thousands of questions each year, many on an emergency basis, in decisions that are "unsigned, and almost always unexplained," and frequently "unseen."[2] Until the mid-2010s, with few exceptions, these cases were

---

[1] Vladeck, *The Shadow Docket: How the Supreme Court Uses Stealth Rulings to Amass Power and Undermine the Republic*, 11.
[2] Vladeck, 13.

J. Novkov (✉)
Rockefeller College of Public Affairs & Policy, University at Albany, SUNY, Albany, NY, USA
e-mail: Jnovkov@albany.edu

little noticed and tended not to address issues with broad national significance.

The Court's emergency docket for the 2024–25 term comprised 113 cases (including some petitions that were consolidated), with the Justices deciding 61 petitions prior to Donald Trump's inauguration on January 20, 2025, and 52 afterward based on the count maintained by SCOTUSBlog.[3] The nature and outcomes of the emergency docket changed dramatically after January 20, with the Trump administration filing numerous petitions and having a high degree of success; petitions involving the administration comprised around 18% of the Court's rulings over the year. The ultimate legal fate of many Trump administration policies remains uncertain, but the Court consistently rejected lower federal courts' near-consensus that the policies at issue are problematic enough to warrant pausing or reversing their implementation while the legal battles play out.

Prior to President Trump's second inauguration emergency petitions were heavily disfavored. In keeping with past practice, the Court denied defendants' challenges to lower courts' rulings on criminal law issues, declined attempts to block executions, and rejected two petitions from President-elect Donald Trump that sought to lift a gag order and stay criminal proceedings against him.[4] The Court also rejected two petitions from the Biden administration: one challenging an injunction that paused new protections for transgender individuals, and another that sought to overturn an order blocking the implementation of student loan debt relief.[5] Aside from two disputes over voting regulations, the Court only granted one emergency petition, which reversed a Fifth Circuit ruling blocking the creation of a nonprofit organization to protect racehorses.[6]

After Trump's inauguration, the Court continued to reject most petitions that did not involve the Trump administration.[7] But the petitions

---

[3] "Emergency Docket 2024." Petitions filed after the end of the Court's term are considered part of the 2025 emergency docket, though the Court did issue July decisions for petitions filed in June.

[4] Good Lawgic, LLC v. Merchan, 145 S. Ct.; Trump v. New York, 145 S. Ct.

[5] Cardona v. Tennessee; Biden v. Missouri, 603 U.S.

[6] Horseracing Integrity and Safety Authority, Inc. v. National Horsemen's Benevolent and Protective Assn., 604 U.S.

[7] One exception was the Court's ruling restoring a Maine state representative's voting rights in the Maine House during a legal dispute over her censure for anti-trans social media posting. *Libby v. Fecteau*, U.S. 605.

that involved the Trump administration were different: the Court granted the administration relief in twenty of twenty-one cases, preventing the implementation of lower court rulings that had blocked the administration from cancelling expenditures, firing federal workers, and deporting unwanted immigrants. The Court issued these rulings mostly as short *per curiam* opinions with little or no legal analysis, or as even briefer unsigned orders. These actions divided the Justices, with only two rulings registering no disagreements. Most of the opposition came from the Court's liberal wing.

Political scientist Adam Bonica described the difference in treatment between the Supreme Court and the lower federal courts as an "open conflict," with federal district courts ruling against the administration nearly 95% of the time from May 1 through June 23 while in the same period the Supreme Court supported the administration in fifteen out of sixteen cases,[8] a trend that has continued thereafter.[9] The pattern is striking, but reading these outcomes as clear evidence that the Supreme Court is in support of Trump's agenda oversimplifies the matter. The administration appealed cases selectively, choosing the best targets for Supreme Court collaboration and opting to allow other lower court rulings to stand or seeking relief through the normal and slower appellate process. The Supreme Court's majority has drawn a sharp boundary between ruling on the preliminary concerns raised in these petitions and ruling on the larger questions of the legitimacy of the administration's actions, which the majority seems to want to defer to some unspecified future date.

IMMIGRATION AND DEPORTATION POLICY

On the six petitions addressed immigration issues, the Trump administration secured full victory in four cases and partial victory in a fifth, with the Court deciding a final case in favor of the petitioning immigrant.

The Trump administration won in two cases that involved stripping legal status from hundreds of thousands of individuals by revoking Temporary Protected Status and terminating humanitarian parole programs. The Temporary Protected Status program was created in 1990 to

---

[8] Bonica, "The Supreme Court vs. The Lower Courts: Rulings on the Trump Administration." Bonica's analysis was completed prior to the Court's high-profile ruling in *Trump v. CASA*.
[9] Vladeck, "Bonus 165: The Appeasement Thesis."

allow protection from deportation for individuals at extraordinary and temporary risk due to conditions in their home countries. Three days after being sworn in, DHS Secretary Kristi Noem cancelled TPS status for more than 600,000 Venezuelans. A lower court blocked the action; in response to an emergency petition the Supreme Court issued an unsigned order overturning the lower court's order, provoking a dissent from Justice Jackson.[10] "Humanitarian parole" allows the Secretary of DHS to allow individuals in urgent humanitarian circumstances to enter and remain in the United States on a temporary basis. Secretary Noem revoked humanitarian parole from more than half a million noncitizens with no provision for case-by-case review. A District Court in Massachusetts blocked the action; again the Supreme Court intervened to stay the lower court's injunction without explanation. Justice Jackson, joined by Justice Sotomayor, dissented.[11]

Another tool for the administration's mass deportation agenda is the Alien Enemies Act of 1798, a little-used statute that enables the detention or deportation of nationals of a country engaged in a military dispute with the United States. A Trump Executive Order deployed the Act to target members of a Venezuelan gang, Tren de Aragua.[12] Removals began quickly and sparked immediate legal challenges. The chief judge of the US District Court for the District of Columbia temporarily barred deportations under the Act, and ordered two planes that were in the air to be returned to the United States. The administration continued the action, claiming that the judge lacked jurisdiction over international airspace.[13] The Court vacated the judge's order but also found that "detainees subject to removal orders under the AEA are entitled to notice and an opportunity to challenge their removal." Subsequently, in a rare rebuff in *A.A.R.P v. Trump*, the Court enjoined removals under the Alien Enemies Act, finding that the administration had failed to provide the plaintiffs with adequate notice when they were provided with only 24 hours' notice and no instruction on how to challenge removal. Justices Alito and Thomas dissented.[14]

---

[10] Noem v. National TPS Alliance, 605 U.S.

[11] Noem v. Doe, 605 U.S.

[12] Treisman, "4 Things to Know about the Alien Enemies Act and Trump's Efforts to Use It."

[13] "Judge Calls DOJ Filing 'Woefully Insufficient' in Legal Standoff over Deportation Flights."

[14] A.A.R.P. v. Trump, 605 U.S.

The Court returned to form, however, in *Department of Homeland Security v. D.V.D.*, when they were asked to stay a ruling that barred DHS from removing individuals to countries not identified in their removal orders. The Court stayed the lower court's injunction, and when the lower court nonetheless tried to prevent the transfer of eight men from a military base in Djibouti to South Sudan, the Court intervened again to lift the legal barrier.[15] Justice Kagan, who had dissented from the first ruling, concurred in the second on the ground that the district court was not empowered to defy the Supreme Court, but Justice Sotomayor, joined by Justice Jackson, dissented.

The exceptional final case—*Noem v. Abrego Garcia*—involved an individual's resistance against Trump deportation policies. Kilmar Abrego Garcia fled gang violence in El Salvador and traveled to Maryland, where he eventually secured protection against deportation. In March 2025, the Trump administration detained and deported him to El Salvador's notorious CECOT prison due to an admitted administrative error.[16] In early April, a Maryland district court judge ordered the administration to "facilitate and effectuate" Abrego Garcia's return to the United States by midnight on the following Monday.[17] The administration asked the Court to lift the injunction, and the Court partially granted this request on April 10 to clarify the scope of the district court's order, warning that "the intended scope of the term 'effectuate' ... is ... unclear, and may exceed the District Court's authority."[18] Justice Sotomayor wrote separately, joined by Justices Kagan and Jackson, to object to the Court having intervened at all.[19] While Abrego Garcia has been returned to the United States (an outcome the administration claimed to be incapable of achieving), the administration has continued to pursue removal strategies.

---

[15] Department of Homeland Security v. D.V.D., 606 U.S.; Department of Homeland Security v. D.V.D. (motion for clarification), 606 U.S.
[16] Finley, "What to Know After Judge Keeps Kilmar Abrego Garcia in Jail Over Deportation Fears."
[17] Abrego Garcia v. Noem, Order Granting Preliminary Injunction.
[18] Noem v. Abrego Garcia, 604 U.S. at 2.
[19] Noem v. Abrego Garcia, 604 U.S. at 3.

Restructuring the Federal Bureaucracy

The administration's efforts to restructure the federal bureaucracy, empower data sharing across administrative units, and reduce the federal workforce have also been met with roadblocks in the lower federal courts that the Supreme Court has proven willing to remove. Eight controversies produced eleven petitions that reached the Court, with the administration scoring significant victories in seven of the controversies, allowing these agendas to advance.

Two petitions involved the cost-cutting entity, DOGE. DOGE affiliates demanded access to Social Security Administration records, including sensitive and confidential personal information. The American Federation of State, County, and Municipal Employees (AFSCME) and others filed suit, claiming that allowing this access would violate the Privacy Act of 1974. Maryland's senior federal district judge agreed, prohibiting the SSA from granting access.[20] In June, the Court stayed the order.[21] The three liberals disagreed with this outcome. In a similar case, The Center for Responsibility and Ethics in Washington (CREW) filed suit in February 2025 against DOGE and other government agencies and agents under the Freedom of Information Act (FOIA) and requested expedited discovery. The federal district court for the District of Columbia largely acceded to CREW's request, but the Supreme Court stayed the lower court's orders without explanation.[22] Again, the three liberal justices objected.

Four petitions involved the administration's efforts to shrink the federal workforce, and three addressed lawsuits initiated by several interest groups and the American Federation of Government Employees (AFGE), the primary union for most federal workers. The Court overturned an injunction that would have temporarily prevented the Office of Personnel Management's (OPM) mass termination of probationary employees in several agencies, with Sotomayor and Jackson registering objection, finding that the not-for-profit organizations had not established standing.[23] A temporary restraining order preventing the administration from pursuing overall reduction in force plans was stayed (Justice Jackson dissenting), and a lower court order requiring the reinstatement of Department of

---

[20] Howe, "Trump Asks High Court to Allow DOGE Access to Social Security Records."
[21] Social Security Administration v. AFSCME, 605 U.S. at 2.
[22] U.S. DOGE Service v. CREW, 605 U.S.
[23] OPM v. AFGE, U.S.

Education employees was stayed without explanation.[24] All three liberals objected. Justice Sotomayor's dissent strongly criticized both the executive branch and the Court: "When the Executive publicly announces its intent to break the law, and then executes on that promise, it is the Judiciary's duty to check that lawlessness, not expedite it."[25]

Two cases involving the executive's authority to remove individuals from independent executive agencies raised larger questions about whether the Court may be ready to reconsider *Humphrey's Executor*, a ninety-year-old precedent that limits a President's ability to remove senior agency officials. One, involving the head of the Office of Special Counsel, was ultimately dismissed as moot.[26] The administration also removed Biden appointees from the Merit Systems Protection Board (MSRB) and the National Labor Relations Board (NLRB). The dismissed employees obtained court orders mandating their reinstatement; the Court stayed the orders, and hinted that at least some members of the Court are inclined to side with the administration on the substantive question. Justice Kagan dissented, joined by Justices Sotomayor and Jackson.[27]

Cancellation of Federal Grants

Two petitions involved administration's cancellation of federal grants. The first challenged the pausing of disbursements of foreign development assistance funds. The District Court for the District of Columbia ordered the government to pay for work that had already been completed. The administration requested that the Supreme Court vacate the order, but the Court declined to do so, instead instructing the district court judge to "clarify what obligations the Government must fulfill."[28] In this victory for administration opponents, Chief Justice Roberts and Justice Barrett sided with the liberals, leaving Justices Alito, Thomas, Gorsuch, and Kavanaugh in dissent. On the other hand, when a Massachusetts judge issued a TRO pausing the termination of grants targeting teacher training, the Court issued a ruling vacating the order.[29] The Chief Justice indicated his

---

[24] McMahon v. New York, 606 U.S.
[25] McMahon v. New York, 606 U.S. at 2.
[26] Blythe, "Why Hampton Dellinger Ended His Legal Battle Against President Trump."
[27] Trump v. Wilcox, 605 U.S.
[28] Department of State v. AIDS Vaccine Advocacy Coalition.
[29] Department of Education v. California, 604 U.S.

disagreement with the majority, and Justice Kagan and Justice Jackson, joined by Justice Sotomayor, wrote separately to dissent.

ADDITIONAL CASES

Significant legal questions were raised in two other cases concerning President Trump's executive orders and their proposed implementation.

In *United States v. Shilling*, the administration challenged a Washington District Court's preliminary injunction that stopped the Department of Defense's effort to oust trans individuals from the military. The Court issued a brief order granting the government's request to pause the injunction while the government's appeal proceeded in the Ninth Circuit, generating objections from the three liberals.[30]

Finally, on his first day in office President Trump issued an Executive Order directing federal agencies to prepare to deny documents acknowledging citizenship to infants of undocumented mothers and lawful temporary residents if they did not have fathers with citizenship or lawful permanent residence. The order proved to be highly unpopular in the federal district courts, collecting temporary restraining orders and injunctions in four states. Unlike most of the other emergency docket rulings, which were issued *per curiam*, the ruling in *Trump v. CASA* identified Justice Barrett as the opinion's author. Justice Barrett's opinion discussed the problematic nature of universal injunctions issued at the district court level and explained that Congress had never granted federal courts the authority to "universally enjoin the enforcement of an executive or legislative policy."[31] The majority found that universal injunctions are not rooted in historical practices of equitable relief and suggested that litigants interested in pursuing broad relief might instead file class action suits.[32] The ruling prompted two in-depth dissents from Justices Sotomayor and Jackson. Justice Sotomayor's dissent addressed the underlying question of the Executive Order's constitutionality, concluding that it was unconstitutional based on the clear meaning of the Fourteenth Amendment's text and history.[33]

---

[30] Howe, "Supreme Court Allows Trump to Ban Transgender People from the Military."
[31] Trump v. CASA, 606 U.S. at 4.
[32] Trump v. CASA, 606 U.S. at 11–13.
[33] Trump v. CASA, 606 U.S. at 1. (Jackson dissenting.)

CONCLUSION

The Court's handling of the 2024–25 emergency docket, particularly since the inauguration of President Trump, provokes important questions about the administration, the Court, and the future of American democracy.

First, the administration's legal team has demonstrated its ability to choose and frame issues to present successfully on an emergency basis, not pressing forward to challenge every loss immediately. The cases it has chosen have been not only successful but also broadly impactful, and the focus has been on getting the policy changes into place. While in some cases the briefs have provided substantive arguments about the legality of the actions, the administration has focused on enabling the policies to go into effect while awaiting the ultimate resolution of challenges based on statutes and the constitution. Individuals and groups challenging these policies have often been unable to convince a majority of the Court that the disruptions and harms are serious enough and that the legal questions are clear enough to warrant maintaining barriers to implementation, while the conservative Justices have treated any disruption of the ability of the administration to immediately pursue its policies as an irreparable harm.

Second is the notable and bitter divide on the Court about the administration's actions and the most appropriate legal response to them. The *per curiam* opinions providing emergency relief to the administration have occasionally emphasized that they are not signaling any commitment to the ultimate fate of the policies being challenged. The majority's stance seems to be that the executive branch should enjoy a great degree of deference, especially when claiming emergency or extraordinary circumstances warrant it. They further seem to be signaling that allowing the ordinary legal process to continue until cases on the merits reach the Court through the appellate process will be sufficient to maintain the rule of law. In contrast, the liberal Justices in dissent, particularly Justices Jackson and Sotomayor, sound an urgent warning about their perceptions of the lawlessness of the Trump administration, the threats that this lawlessness poses for American democracy and the victims of potentially illegal action, and the need to intervene immediately to interrupt a slide toward authoritarianism.

Third, the actions and reasoning of the majority raise questions about their take on the Trump administration. Justices Alito and Thomas seem to be signaling their support for at least some aspects of the administration's agendas. The other Justices' willingness to grant emergency relief, presumably led by Chief Justice Roberts, could signal three different viewpoints that the majority collectively or individually embrace. One is the idea expressed above that the administration's actions, while unusual, are not extraordinarily threatening and therefore do not warrant the extraordinarily negative response they have garnered in the lower federal courts. The second is that the majority is waiting for the right case to deliver a rebuke to the administration, and perhaps may not be willing to do so until they have a developed ruling on the merits with a full record below. John Roberts, as a student of the Court's history, has contributed significantly to the Court's empowerment during his tenure as Chief and is likely well aware of the risks of issuing a ruling that the executive branch will defy or ignore. Waiting for the right case may for the majority be a tactic to ensure the Court's continued empowerment and legitimacy in the eyes of the American public. The third is that the majority is stalling in the hope that Congress will solve these serious conflicts after the midterm elections, or that the Court itself will be able to intervene to uphold the rule of law triumphantly after the ordinary slow pace of litigation brings key questions to them after Trump has left office.

A final note, however, is that the Court's empowerment mission is clearly continuing, but has migrated into a new area: the majority's insistence that only the Supreme Court, not the lower federal courts, should have the final say on how and when federal policies will be implemented nationally. And at least in those instances where the policy agendas of the Court and the Trump administration align, this stance will likely contribute to lasting changes in American politics and policy.

CHAPTER 5

A.A.R.P. v. Trump: The Uncertain Future of Presidential Power in Removal Cases

Jonathan Hafetz and David L. Sloss

On March 14, 2025, President Trump issued a proclamation under the Alien Enemies Act (AEA) declaring that certain members of Tren de Aragua (TdA), an entity designated as a foreign terrorist organization, "are subject to immediate apprehension, detention, and removal" from the United States. The plan for summary removal under the AEA applies to "all Venezuelan citizens 14 years of age or older who are members of TdA, are within the United States, and are not actually naturalized or lawful permanent residents of the United States."[1]

---

[1] Presidential Proclamation No. 10903, 90 Fed Reg. 13033 (2025).

J. Hafetz (✉)
Seton Hall Law School, Newark, NJ, USA
e-mail: Jonathan.hafetz@shu.edu

D. L. Sloss
University of Santa Clara Law School, Santa Clara, CA, USA
e-mail: dlsloss@scu.edu

© The Author(s), under exclusive license to Springer Nature Switzerland AG 2026
H. Schweber (ed.), *SCOTUS 2025*,
https://doi.org/10.1007/978-3-032-10231-7_5

The Supreme Court's May 2025 decision in *A.A.R.P. v. United States* arose from a habeas petition filed by two Venezuelan nationals whom the government had targeted for summary removal.[2] Previously, in April 2025, the Court held in *Trump v. J.G.G.* that, under the Fifth Amendment Due Process Clause, detainees subject to removal under the AEA "must receive notice ... that they are subject to removal under the Act," and that such "notice must be afforded ... in such a manner as will allow them to actually seek habeas relief in the proper venue before such removal occurs."[3]

The petitioners in *A.A.R.P.* claimed that the government was denying them the Fifth Amendment due process rights that the Court had promised in *J.G.G.* In a *per curiam* decision, the Supreme Court ruled in favor of the petitioners. It said: "Under these circumstances, notice roughly 24 hours before removal, devoid of information about how to exercise due process rights to contest that removal, surely does not pass muster." It remanded the case to the Fifth Circuit "to determine in the first instance the precise process necessary to satisfy the Constitution in this case."[4]

This essay briefly reviews the series of events between the President's March 14 proclamation and the Court's May 16 decision in *A.A.R.P*, including the Court's prior decision in *J.G.G.* It then analyzes the main issues presented in *A.A.R.P.* The final section presents some brief reflections on the potential broader implications of litigation challenging the removal of Venezuelan nationals under the AEA and its connection to a disturbing pattern of government attempts to evade due process and circumvent judicial orders in immigration cases.

Background

The Alien Enemies Act (AEA), originally enacted in 1798, provides as follows:

> Whenever there is a declared war between the United States and any foreign nation or government, or any invasion or predatory incursion is perpetrated, attempted, or threatened against the territory of the United States by any foreign nation or government, and the President makes public proclamation

---

[2] A.A.R.P v. Trump, 145 S. Ct. 1364 (2025).
[3] Trump v. J.G.G., 145 S. Ct. 1003, 1006 (2025).
[4] A.A.R.P v. Trump, 145 S. Ct. at 1368.

of the event, all natives, citizens, denizens, or subjects of the hostile nation or government, being of the age of fourteen years and upward, who shall be within the United States and not actually naturalized, shall be liable to be apprehended, restrained, secured, and removed as alien enemies.[5]

Under the statute, foreigners are removable under the AEA (absent a declared war) only if: (1) there is an "invasion or predatory incursion," (2) carried out "by any foreign nation or government." Accordingly, President Trump stated in his proclamation "that TdA is perpetrating, attempting, and threatening an invasion or predatory incursion against the territory of the United States," and that TdA is acting "at the direction, clandestine or otherwise, of the Maduro regime in Venezuela."[6] These statements in the proclamation provide the factual predicates for the determination that TdA members are removable under the AEA.

Habeas petitioners have filed petitions in several different district courts challenging the lawfulness of the President's proclamation. Petitioners argue that the proclamation exceeds the scope of the President's statutory authority because, as a factual matter, there is no "invasion or predatory incursion" and TdA is not acting as an agent of the Government of Venezuela. As of this writing, four federal district courts have addressed the merits of these claims. Judge Rodriguez, a Trump appointee, concluded that the "President's invocation of the AEA through the Proclamation exceeds the scope of the statute and is contrary to the plain, ordinary meaning of the statute's terms."[7] Similarly, Judge Sweeney, a Biden appointee, concluded that "Petitioners are likely to succeed on the merits of their claim that the President's invocation of the Act through the Proclamation exceeds the scope of the statute and is therefore unlawful."[8] Judge Hellerstein, a Clinton appointee, reached a similar conclusion.[9] In contrast, Judge Haines, a Trump appointee, concluded that the President's proclamation is lawful, and that the AEA provides statutory authorization for removal of TdA members.[10]

As of this writing, the Supreme Court has not reached the merits of those claims. Nor has it decided the contours of due process guarantees

[5] Act of July 6, 1798, ch. 66, §1, 1 Stat. 577 (codified at 50 U.S.C. § 21).
[6] Presidential Proclamation No. 10903, 90 Fed Reg. 13033 (2025).
[7] J.A.V. v. Trump, 2025 WL 1257450, at *1 (S.D. Tex., May 1, 2025).
[8] D.B.U. v. Trump, 2025 WL 1304288, at *7 (D. Colo., May 6, 2025).
[9] G.F.F. v. Trump, 2025 WL 1301052 (S.D.N.Y., May 6, 2025).
[10] A.S.R. v. Trump, 2025 WL 1385213 (W.D. PA., May 13, 2025).

that would apply to individuals challenging their removal under the AEA, assuming the proclamation is valid.

Trump v. J.G.G. was the first case to reach the Court. In that case, five Venezuelan nationals sued in federal court in the District of Columbia. They filed claims under the Administrative Procedure Act (APA) to challenge the legality of removal under the AEA.[11] On March 15 (the day after the President's proclamation, which had not yet been disclosed to the public even though the government had reportedly initiated operations to remove "scores of Venezuelans" by placing them on planes),[12] Judge Boasberg provisionally certified a class of noncitizens who were detained pursuant to the President's proclamation. He issued two temporary restraining orders, barring removal of the named plaintiffs and barring removal of other class members based on the President's proclamation without a prior judicial hearing.[13]

On April 7, the Supreme Court vacated the TROs. In a 5–4 decision in *Trump v. J.G.G.*, the Court held that detainees' claims "fall within the 'core' of the writ of habeas corpus and thus must be brought in habeas."[14] Moreover, the Court added: "For core habeas petitions, jurisdiction lies only in one district: the district of confinement."[15] The immediate effect of the Court's decision was thus to deprive Judge Boasberg of jurisdiction to adjudicate the APA claims filed in the District of Columbia, and to force the *J.G.G.* plaintiffs to file habeas petitions in the various districts where they were being confined. In a separate paragraph of the Court's opinion, which was unanimous, the Court also held that "AEA detainees must receive notice … that they are subject to removal under the Act." Moreover, such "notice must be afforded within a reasonable time and in such manner as will allow them to actually seek habeas relief in the proper venue before such removal occurs."[16]

---

[11] *See* J.G.G. v. Trump, 2025 WL 890401 (D.D.C., March 24, 2025).
[12] J.G.G. v. Trump, 2025 WL 1119481, *2 (D.D.C. Apr. 16, 2025).
[13] J.G.G. v. Trump, 2025 WL 890401.
[14] Trump v. J.G.G., 145 S. Ct. 1003, 1005 (2025).
[15] *Id.* at 1005–06.
[16] *Id.* at 1006.

The Habeas Petition in *A.A.R.P. v. Trump*

The Court's opinion in *Trump v. J.G.G.* sparked a flurry of activity in which Venezuelan nationals detained pursuant to the President's proclamation—as well as those at risk of future removal under the AEA—filed habeas petitions in the districts where they were being confined. The government had detained two of the five named plaintiffs in *J.G.G.* in the Northern District of Texas. Those two, A.A.R.P. and W.M.M., filed suit on behalf of a putative class of similarly situated detainees in that district. On April 17, 2025, the district court denied their motion for a temporary restraining order (TRO) against summary removal under the AEA. Within hours after the court's ruling, the government served them notices of removal and informed them that they would be removed from the United States "tonight or tomorrow."[17]

Then, at 12:34 AM central time on April 18, petitioners moved for an emergency TRO. The district court did not act on that motion. At 3:02 PM the same day, petitioners filed an appeal with the Fifth Circuit to challenge the "constructive denial" of the emergency TRO. The Fifth Circuit promptly dismissed that appeal for lack of jurisdiction. Petitioners applied to the Supreme Court for a temporary injunction. Meanwhile, the government had "taken steps on the afternoon of April 18 toward removing detainees under the AEA—including transporting them from their detention facility to an airport."[18] The Supreme Court later said that it "understood the Government to assert the right to remove the detainees as soon as midnight central time on April 19."[19] In that context, given the rapidly evolving situation, at 11:52 PM central time on April 18 (shortly after midnight, Eastern Time), the Court ordered the government "not to remove any member of the putative class of detainees" in order to preserve the Court's jurisdiction to consider the habeas petition.[20]

Here, it is worth noting the related case of Kilmar Abrego Garcia, a Maryland resident whom the government had deported to El Salvador due to what the government admitted was "an administrative error."[21] On

---

[17] A.A.R.P. v. Trump, 145 S. Ct. at 1366.
[18] *Id.*, at 1367.
[19] *Id.*, at 1366.
[20] A.A.R.P. v. Trump, 145 S. Ct. 1034 (Mem) (Apr. 19, 2025).
[21] *See* NBC News, What we Know about Kilmar Abrego Garcia (Apr. 21, 2025), https://www.nbcnews.com/news/us-news/kilmar-abrego-garcia-deported-el-salvador-trump-immigration-what-know-rcna201708.

April 7, in a judicial proceeding in the *Abrego Garcia* case, the government argued that no U.S. court had jurisdiction to order his return from El Salvador to the United States. Then, on April 14, in a widely publicized White House meeting between President Trump and Nayib Bukele (the President of El Salvador), President Bukele stated publicly that he would not return Abrego Garcia to the United States.[22] The Court was mindful of these events when it issued its emergency order shortly after midnight, Eastern Time, on April 19. Indeed, when the Court issued its opinion in *A.A.R.P.* a few weeks later, it cited the government's statement in *Abrego Garcia* as part of its rationale for issuing the emergency order on April 19 "to preserve our jurisdiction to consider the application."[23]

Approximately four weeks after issuing its midnight order, the Court released an opinion in *A.A.R.P.* to explain the rationale for its unusually hasty decision on April 18–19. The Court divided 7–2 in *A.A.R.P.* Justice Alito filed a dissenting opinion on behalf of himself and Justice Thomas. The unsigned, majority opinion touches upon three distinct issues: the Court's jurisdiction, the requirements of due process, and the reasons for ordering relief on behalf of a putative class that had not been certified.

First, the Court held that "the Fifth Circuit erred in dismissing the detainees' appeal for lack of jurisdiction." The Court noted that "appellate courts have jurisdiction to review interlocutory orders that have the practical effect of refusing an injunction." In *A.A.R.P*, the Court had jurisdiction because "the District Court's inaction—not for 42 minutes but for 14 hours and 28 minutes—had the practical effect of refusing an injunction to detainees facing an imminent threat of severe, irreparable harm."[24] Specifically, there was a threat of irreparable harm because, absent an injunction, the government might have sent them to El Salvador, where they could be detained indefinitely without any opportunity for a judicial hearing and, in light of the government's position in *Abrego Garcia*, without any possibility of a remedy.[25] Justices Alito and Thomas disagreed, largely because, in their view, "the District Court had no good reason to

---

[22] *See* NBC News, El Salvador's President Says He Won't Return Mistakenly Deported Man to U.S. (April 14, 2025), https://www.nbcnews.com/politics/trump-administration/president-el-salvador-wont-return-deported-man-kilmar-abrego-garcia-rcna201136.

[23] A.A.R.P. v. Trump, 145 S. Ct. at 1367.

[24] *Id.*

[25] *Id.* at 1368 (citing *Abrego Garcia*).

think that either A.A.R.P or W.M.M. was in imminent danger of removal."[26]

The Court's opinion in *A.A.R.P.* did not break any new ground on procedural due process. It reiterated the familiar refrain that "the Fifth Amendment entitles aliens to due process of law in the context of removal proceedings."[27] And it quoted *J.G.G.* for the proposition that "AEA detainees must receive notice ... that they are subject to removal under the Act ... within a reasonable time and in such a manner as will allow them to actually seek habeas relief" before removal. The Court added: "In order to 'actually seek habeas relief,' a detainee must have sufficient time and information to reasonably be able to contact counsel, file a petition, and pursue appropriate relief."[28] (The dissenting Justices did not challenge this portion of the Court's opinion.) The majority concluded that the government's conduct in this case—providing "notice roughly 24 hours before removal, devoid of information about how to exercise due process rights to contest that removal"—did not satisfy Fifth Amendment requirements.[29] The Court remanded the case to the Fifth Circuit "to determine in the first instance the precise process necessary to satisfy the Constitution in this case."[30]

The dissenting Justices challenged the idea that class relief is available in habeas proceedings. Justice Alito wrote: "We have never so held, and it is highly questionable whether it is permitted."[31] The majority opinion walked a delicate tightrope on this issue. The Court ducked the question whether class certification is appropriate and acknowledged that different members of the putative class may have divergent interests to some extent. However, it insisted: "The named applicants, along with putative class members, are entitled to constitutionally adequate notice prior to any removal ... [and] the notice to which they are entitled is the same."[32] Therefore, the Court concluded, for the purpose of interim relief (as opposed to final relief), it is appropriate "to temporarily enjoin the

---

[26] *Id.* at 1371 (Alito, J., dissenting).
[27] *Id.*, at 1367 (per curiam).
[28] *Id.*, at 1368.
[29] As plaintiffs-petitioners had argued, the notice, for example, was provided to detainees only in English, a language many did not speak or understand. *See* A.A.R.P. v. Trump, No. 24A1007, Reply in Support of Emergency Application, at 5.
[30] A.A.R.P. v. Trump, 145 S. Ct. at 1368.
[31] *Id.*, at 1375 (Alito, J., dissenting).
[32] *Id.*, at 1369 (per curiam).

Government from removing putative class members while the question of what notice is due is adjudicated."[33] In short, before a class has been properly certified, and even though class certification may ultimately be denied, the Fifth Amendment guarantees due process rights for all putative class members, and a temporary injunction is appropriate to help ensure that no class member is denied his/her constitutional rights.

BROADER IMPLICATIONS

The Court's decision in *A.A.R.P.* leaves open several unresolved questions. First, there remains the substantive question whether Trump's proclamation is valid, an issue the Supreme Court may confront next Term. To decide that question, the Court will have to determine whether there is (1) an "invasion or predatory incursion"; (2) that is carried out "by [a] foreign nation or government." In the past, the AEA has been invoked only during wartime. It has also been invoked only against enemy states. The Trump administration argues, however, that the TdA is "conducting irregular warfare and undertaking hostile actions" against the United States and is operating in conjunction with a narco-terrorism enterprise in Venezuela that is sponsored by President Nicolas Maduro.[34] Thus far, nearly all lower courts to address the issue have at least preliminarily found that the proclamation exceeds the AEA's scope, concluding that an "invasion or predatory incursion" requires some form of armed attack or entry of an armed force into the United States.[35] The issue is now pending before the Fifth Circuit.[36] If the Supreme Court ultimately validates the proclamation, it would mark a significant expansion of the AEA and create a precedent for the statute's future use as an immigration-control measure.

The Court will also likely be asked to flesh out the contours of due process requirements. Following the Court's initial order in *A.A.R.P.*, a federal judge in the Western District of Pennsylvania concluded that

---

[33] *Id.*
[34] Presidential Proclamation No. 10903, *supra* note 1.
[35] *See* J.G.G. v. Trump, 2025 WL 914682 at *8–10 (D.C. Cir., Mar. 26, 2025) (Henderson, J., concurring); G.F.F. v. Trump, No. 25-cv 2886, 2025 WL 1301052, at *9–10 (S.D.N.Y. May 6, 2025); D.B.U. v. Trump, No. 25-cv-01163, 2025 WL 1304288, at *6 (D. Colo. May 6, 2025); J.A.V. v. Trump, No. 1:25-cv-072, 2025 WL 1257450, at *15–16 (S.D. Tex. May 1, 2025).
[36] The Fifth Circuit held argument on June 30, 2025. *See* W.M.M. v. Trump, No. 25-10534 (5th Cir. 2025).

detainees are entitled to 21 days' notice, in a language the detainee understands, that they are subject to removal under the act.[37] The judge rejected the administration's claim that this requirement would unduly burden the government.[38] Because other lower courts rejected President Trump's invocation of the proclamation as a threshold matter, they have not addressed these types of procedural issues.

The interplay between substance (i.e., validity of the proclamation) and procedure (i.e., process to determine whether an individual is an alien enemy) could also affect the outcome. The AEA litigation could, for example, follow the Guantanamo habeas litigation, which addressed the President's power to detain enemy combatants under the 2001 Authorization for Use of Military Force (AUMF).[39] There, the Court insisted on some limited process in individual habeas cases[40] without directly challenging the President's claim of broad detention authority, even as that authority was stretched beyond traditional wartime parameters to reach nonstate actors across the globe with minimal nexus to a combat zone.[41] Were the Court to allow removals under the proclamation to proceed—even accompanied by due process—it would mark another significant expansion of executive power under a wartime mantle, allowing a President to treat migrants akin to an invading army rather than addressing migration exclusively through a civilian law enforcement framework. This powerful new tool, moreover, could be extended to migrants from other countries, much as the AUMF was expanded beyond those directly implicated in the 9/11 attacks.[42]

The AEA litigation also underscores concerns about government noncompliance with judicial orders. In *J.G.G.*, the government removed some individuals pursuant to the President's proclamation in violation of a district court order temporarily enjoining such transfers.[43] In April 2025, Judge Boasberg ruled that the government had demonstrated a willful

---

[37] A.S.R. v. Trump, 3:25-cv-00113-SLH, at 35–36 (W.D. Pa. May 13, 2025).

[38] *Id.* at 36.

[39] Pub. L. No. 107-40, 115 Stat. 224.

[40] *See* Boumediene v. Bush, 553 US 723 (2008); Rasul v. Bush, 542 U.S. 466 (2005).

[41] See Curtis A. Bradley & Jack L. Goldsmith, "Obama's AUMF Legacy," 110 *Am. J. Int'l L.* 628, 630 (2016).

[42] See Harold Hongju Koh, "Ending the Forever War: One Year After President Obama's NDU Speech," *Just Security* (May 23, 2014), https://www.justsecurity.org/10768/harold-koh-forever-war-president-obama-ndu-speech/.

[43] J.G.G. v. Trump, No. 25-766 (JEB), 2025 WL 1119481, at *3–*5 (Apr. 16, 2025).

disregard for the court's temporary restraining order and concluded that there was probable cause to find the government in criminal contempt.[44] The D.C. Circuit, however, stayed Judge Boasberg's ruling pending appeal.[45]

Another immigration case from this Term, *Department of Homeland Security v. D.V.D.*,[46] is also instructive. *D.V.D.* addressed the issue whether the United States may remove an individual to a country other than the one identified in their original order of removal, without first providing them an opportunity to challenge the "third-country removal" based on a risk of torture in that third country. A district court barred the government from removing a class of noncitizens to third countries without notice and an opportunity to be heard.[47] But on June 23, 2025, the Supreme Court stayed that ruling in an unsigned order and without explanation.[48] Justice Sotomayor noted in a vigorous dissent, joined by Justices Kagan and Jackson, that depriving individuals of any meaningful opportunity to challenge their removal to a country where they risked torture effectively nullifies "Congress's carefully calibrated scheme of immigration law," which provides a statutory right to challenge removals on those grounds.[49]

Although the statutory schemes in the cases are different, the Court's issuance of the stay in *D.V.D.* is difficult to square with its rulings in *A.A.R.P.* and *J.G.G.*, which insisted on notice and an opportunity to be heard *before* the government removes people from the country. Like the AEA cases, moreover, *D.V.D.* raises questions about noncompliance with court orders, given that the government apparently removed some individuals to third countries in violation of the district court's order[50]—precisely the type of misconduct that Justice Sotomayor said should have prompted the Court to refuse the government's request for emergency relief.[51] Thus, if *A.A.R.P.* demonstrates the Court's determination to

---

[44] *Id.* at *1.
[45] J.G.G. v. Trump, No. 25-5124, 2025 WL 1151208 (D.C. Cir. Apr. 18, 2025).
[46] Department of Homeland Security v. D.V.D., 145 S. Ct. 2153, 2025 WL 1732103 (June 23, 2025).
[47] Department of Homeland Security v. D.V.D., 25-10676-BEM, 2025 WL 1142968, at *1 (D. Mass. Apr. 18, 2025).
[48] Department of Homeland Security v. D.V.D., 2025 WL 1732103.
[49] *Id.* at 8.
[50] *Id.* at *6.
[51] *Id.*

ensure at least some due process is provided before removing a person from the United States, *D.V.D.* suggests the limits of the Court's willingness to constrain the Trump administration's plans to conduct mass deportations.

CHAPTER 6

Trump v. CASA (2025): Birthright Citizenship vs. Universal Injunctions

H. L. Pohlman

On January 29, 2025, President Trump issued an Executive Order that denied citizenship to many children born in the United States if their mothers were unlawfully or temporarily in the United States (e.g., on a student or tourist visa).[1] Citizens Assisting and Sheltering the Abused (CASA), Asylum Support Appeals Project (ASAP), several pregnant women, and 22 states challenged the constitutionality of the Order. After three district courts issued universal injunctions that applied nationwide (not just to the parties of the case), and three federal appellate courts upheld them, Trump applied to the Supreme Court for a stay of the

---

[1] *Protecting the Meaning and Value of American Citizenship*, Exec. Order No. 14, 160, 90 Fed. reg 8449 (January 29, 2025), available at https://www.whitehouse.gov/presidential-actions/2025/01/protecting-the-meaning-and-value-of-american-citizenship/.

H. L. Pohlman (✉)
Political Science, Professor Emeritus, Dickinson College, Carlisle, PA, USA
e-mail: Pohlman@dickinson.edu

© The Author(s), under exclusive license to Springer Nature Switzerland AG 2026
H. Schweber (ed.), *SCOTUS 2025*,
https://doi.org/10.1007/978-3-032-10231-7_6

universal injunctions on the ground that they were unconstitutional.[2] The case pitted one controversial constitutional question against another: "Does Trump have the unilateral constitutional authority to deny citizenship to these children despite the legal tradition of U.S. birthright citizenship?" versus "Do federal judges have the constitutional authority to issue universal injunctions?" On June 27, 2025, the Supreme Court handed down a 6–3 decision that adroitly sidestepped both constitutional questions by holding that Congress never granted federal courts the authority to issue universal injunctions. Although this decision formally relied solely on statutory interpretation, *Trump v. CASA* will undoubtedly have a significant impact on the American constitutional framework by shifting power from the lower federal judiciary to the Executive Branch. Only future Supreme Court decisions will tell us the extent of the shift.

The Merits: Birthright Citizenship

The Citizenship Clause of the Fourteenth Amendment (1868) reads as follows: "All persons born or naturalized in the United States, and **subject to the jurisdiction thereof**, are citizens of the United States and of the State wherein they reside" (emphasis added). Trump's position is that children of mothers unlawfully or temporarily in the United States are not subject to the "political jurisdiction" of the United States and, for that reason, cannot be citizens regardless of their place of birth. In support of this claim, Trump cites the following statement of Senator Trumbull, one of the sponsors of the Fourteenth Amendment: "What do we mean by 'subject to the jurisdiction of the United States?' Not owing allegiance to anybody else. That is what it means."[3] Consistent with this statement, children of foreign diplomats, alien enemies, and tribal Indians born inside the United States were historically excluded from US citizenship. The Supreme Court's decision in *U.S. v. Wong Kim Ark* (1898), which held that a child born in the United States of subjects of the Emperor of China is nonetheless a citizen, was consistent with the Order, Trump argued, because the child's Chinese parents had a "lawful and permanent domicile

---

[2] A "stay" is a legal ruling that temporarily halts judicial actions or proceedings, such as an injunction.

[3] *Trump v. CASA*, Application for a Partial Stay of the Injunction … at 6–7, available at https://www.supremecourt.gov/DocketPDF/24/24A884/352051/20250313135341225_Trump%20v.%20CASA%20Inc%20application.pdf.

and residence" in the United States. Such child would now be called a child of lawful permanent residents. Such children are citizens because it is reasonable to assume that their parents have the requisite political allegiance to the United States.[4] The same cannot be said for children of parents who unlawfully enter or are visiting the United States.

Trump's Application admits that the Executive branch adopted an incorrect understanding of the Citizenship Clause during the twentieth century, extending citizenship to "children of illegal aliens or temporarily present aliens." This policy change "has created strong incentives for illegal immigration," including "birth tourism, the practice by which expecting mothers travel to the United States to give birth and secure U.S. citizenship for their children." It has also raised serious "national-security concerns by extending U.S. citizenship to persons who lack meaningful ties to the country." Trump's Citizenship Order is an attempt to correct this erroneous twentieth-century understanding of US citizenship.[5]

In contrast, CASA's brief in opposition to the stay insists that the relevant phrase—"subject to the jurisdiction thereof"—has "its ordinary meaning, not a special secret one." Accordingly, a person subject to the jurisdiction of the United States is anyone "subject to U.S. power," which would include anyone born inside the United States, excluding three well-known common-law exceptions: children of foreign ministers, occupying armies, and tribal Indians. Trump's reading of *U.S. v. Wong Kim Ark* is simply wrong. The Court held that the child was nonetheless a US citizen even if—contrary to Trump's assumption—the primary allegiance of the Chinese parents was to China's Emperor, not the United States. Trump's claim that the parents' long-term domicile in the United States changed their child's citizenship status cannot be squared with either the "text of the Citizenship Clause or preratification legal authorities." The only relevant factor was place of birth, not allegiance or length of domicile.[6]

CASA cites a string of twentieth-century precedents in support of its understanding of birthright citizenship and emphasizes that Congress codified this understanding in the Nationality Act of 1940, which included

---

[4] *Id*. at 9.
[5] *Id. at 10*.
[6] *Trump v. CASA* (2025), Opposition to Application for a Partial Stay ... at. 5–9, available at https://www.supremecourt.gov/DocketPDF/24/24A884/354782/20250404123331953_CASA%20v%20Trump%20SCOTUS%20Stay%20Opposition%20-%204.4.2025%20-%20to%20file.pdf.

a provision that specifically identified a "person born in the United States, and subject to the jurisdiction thereof" as a "national" and "citizen" of the "United States at birth." CASA cites a report FDR submitted to Congress that maintained it is "the fact of birth within the territory and jurisdiction [of the U.S.], not the domicile of the parents, which determines the nationality of the child." The House sponsor of the legislation agreed, stating on the record that "There are others who, through accident of birth and circumstances have been born in the United States of alien parents, yet can claim citizenship." In addition, a statute enacted in 1952 identified children born in the territories of Alaska and Hawaii as citizens of the United States without any reference to "U.S. jurisdiction." Since there "is no reason to think Congress intended to treat children born in Alaska and Hawaii differently from children born in other states," it follows that Congress intended to codify the "ordinary public meaning" of birthright citizenship. Accordingly, Trump's Order violates not only the Fourteenth Amendment, but also at least two federal statutes.[7]

THE REMEDY: UNIVERSAL INJUNCTIONS

President Trump argues that universal injunctions violate the Constitution because Article III, which delineates the structure and powers of the federal judiciary, limits judicial power to deciding "cases" and "controversies." The three district judges who issued universal injunctions that shielded nonparties from enforcement of the Order were not deciding a "case" or a "controversy," but rather were assuming "a position of authority over the governmental acts of another and co-equal [Executive] department, an authority which plainly [courts] do not possess." Secondly, Article III requires that each party show an "injury" to have the necessary "standing" to bring a case. But the named parties in this case do not have standing to seek relief for nonparties because they cannot "sufficiently answer the question: 'What's it to you?'" After all, there may be parents and children in the two groups that Trump's order excludes from citizenship who do not wish to be US citizens and are therefore in no sense suffering any type of injury. Lastly, universal injunctions "subvert" the Article III hierarchy of the federal judiciary by "imbuing the orders of courts of

---

[7] *Id.* 10–12, 9–11. Nationality Act codified at 8 U.S.C. § 1401(a). See also §1404 (Alaska) and § 1405 (Hawaii) and Notes. Later statehood provisions did not repeal, amend, or modify either provision (See Notes).

first instance [the district courts] with the type of nationwide effect usually reserved for the precedents of the court of last resort [the Supreme Court]."[8]

Trump's Application also insists that universal injunctions infringe Article II of the Constitution, which delineates the structure and power of the Executive Branch, because they invite "forum shopping" that burdens the Executive Branch with constant and fruitless litigation. If plaintiffs do not obtain a universal injunction in one district court, for example, they can simply move on to another court and re-try the same arguments, hoping at some point to get the universal relief they seek. The Executive Branch is left playing a game of whack-a-mole in district after district and, if it loses once, it has lost the game, while the plaintiffs have only to win once to get universal relief. In addition, the injunctions bar executive agencies from issuing "public guidance" regarding enforcement of the Order, thereby violating Article II by "superintend[ing] the Executive Branch's internal operations," a role district courts are clearly not permitted to do.[9]

In response, CASA argues that the universal injunctions are appropriate because the organizational plaintiffs (CASA and ASAP) have approximately 900,000 members that reside in all 50 states. It would be absurd to require each of these members to be a named party of the case. It would also be "burdensome, inefficient, and unworkable" to enjoin enforcement of Trump's Order against children born in the United States of these members, but not other children born in the United States. Federal agencies have no ability to identify with confidence whether a mother unlawfully or temporarily in the United States is a member of one of these associations or not.[10] And, without a universal injunction, different states and regions of the country would likely operate under conflicting standards of citizenship, "An infant would be a United States citizen and full member of society if born in New Jersey, but a deportable noncitizen if born in Tennessee." An additional complication is that, if Trump's order would go into partial effect, then a birth certificate could no longer be sufficient proof of US citizenship "no matter whether a child's parents are citizens or noncitizens."[11] The chaos would be heightened exponentially

---

[8] *Trump v. CASA*, Application for a Partial Stay of the Injunction … at 16–20.
[9] *Id.* at 32–33.
[10] *Trump v. CASA* (2025), Opposition to Application for a Partial Stay … at 22–25.
[11] *Id.* at 20–21

if Trump decided to apply his Order retroactively. No one's birth certificate would suffice, neither one's own nor the birth certificates of one's parents or grandparents; each American citizen would have to prove that his or her parents did not unlawfully enter the country or were not visiting the United States temporarily when he or she was born. The result would be a nightmare.[12]

Second, a universal injunction is appropriate because Trump's Order is "facially" unconstitutional in that there is no set of facts existing anywhere in the United States where it could be constitutionally enforced. This is so because the district courts that issued the universal injunctions "merely applied this Court's binding decision in *Wong Kim Ark*," a Supreme Court precedent that constitutes "controlling precedent throughout the Nation." In the same vein, Trump's Order clearly ignored the Nationality Act of 1940, which is legally binding across the nation. Lastly, enjoining executive agencies from issuing "public guidance" does not violate Article II by "superintend[ing] the Executive Branch's internal operations," but only prohibits the publication of the results of those "internal operations."[13]

The Supreme Court's Decision

In her majority opinion for the Court, Justice Barret offered the following explanation why Trump was entitled to a stay. First, she held that Trump was likely to "succeed on the merits." She came to this somewhat surprising conclusion by limiting the merits of the case to whether universal injunctions were lawful, thereby completely setting aside the issue of whether Trump's Order itself was either constitutional or legal. Next, Barrett adopted a strict historical approach to decide whether universal injunctions were authorized. Although Barret acknowledged that equity was "flexible," she insisted that it was "not freewheeling" and that Congress, in the Judiciary Act of 1789, only intended to give the federal judiciary equitable remedies "that the [British] High Court of Chancery possessed"—of which universal injunctions were not one. The exclusion of this remedy was the reason why the "universal injunction was conspicuously nonexistent for most of our Nation's history," not appearing at all "until sometime in the 20th century," and then only "rarely." It did not become more routine until the twenty-first century, with three-quarters of

---

[12] *Id.* at 21–22.
[13] *Id.* at 25–26, 18, 36–37.

the total number of universal injunctions (96) issued after 2001. For Barrett and the majority, it was this absence of universal injunctions "from the 18th- and 19th-century equity practice [that] settles the question of judicial authority." Since universal injunctions were not permitted then, they are not permitted today.[14]

Second, Barret finds that Trump is entitled to a stay because, without one, his administration will suffer an "irreparable harm": "When a federal court enters a universal injunction against the Government, it 'improper[ly] intrud[es]' on 'a coordinate branch of the Government' and prevents the Government from enforcing its policies against nonparties. That is enough to justify interim relief." To rule otherwise, in Barrett's view, would be a step in the direction of "an Imperial Judiciary." Of course, by basing her finding of an irreparable harm on her earlier conclusion that federal district courts do not have statutory authority to issue universal injunctions, she virtually collapses the two issues into one: The nonexistence of universal injunctions in the eighteenth and nineteenth centuries is proof that they would lead to an "Impaired Executive" as well as an "Imperial judiciary." Barrett concludes that the district court injunctions must exclude nonparties and must not be "broader than necessary to provide complete relief to each plaintiff **with standing to sue**" [emphasis added]. By underlining the necessity of "standing," Barrett sends back to the district courts the question whether Trump's Order "injures" the 22 states and the two associations (CASA and ASAP) in a way that permits them to sue on behalf of all their residents or all their members. Obviously, if district courts deny "standing" to the associations and states, it will significantly narrow the class of parties involved in this litigation as well as broaden the preliminary reach of Trump's Order, stripping citizenship from many who sincerely think of themselves as US citizens.[15]

Barrett says little to nothing regarding the other two standard criteria that an applicant for a stay must meet: whether the stay will substantially injure other interested parties and whether it would serve the public interest.[16] This omission is noteworthy because both seem to implicate the

---

[14] *Trump v. CASA*, No. 24A884, slip. op. at 5–6, 10 (Supreme Court June 27.2025), available at https://www.supremecourt.gov/opinions/24pdf/24a884_8n59.pdf. (Hereafter *Trump v. CASA*).

[15] *Id*. at 24, 23, 26.

[16] The Supreme Court recently endorsed the four requirements for a stay in *Social Security Administration v. American Federation of State, County, and Municipal Employees* (*SSA v. AFSCME*), 605 U.S. ___ (2025), June 6, 2025, at 1–2 (available at https://www.suprem-

merits of Trump's Order: there are obviously nonparties who will be injured if the Court grants the stay, and there is no way the Order could serve the public interest if, as CASA argues, it is unconstitutional. Barrett does acknowledge that there are legitimate policy concerns on both sides, but she sets them aside with the observation that, "as with most questions of law, the policy pros and cons are beside the point."[17] Based on such reasoning, the illicitly broad scope of the universal remedy triumphed over the troubled merits of Trump's Citizenship Order.

Barrett does allow, however, that there are remedies other than universal injunctions potentially available to district courts. First, she mentions the option of class actions lawsuits, allowing one or several plaintiffs to sue on behalf of an entire class of persons, but at the same time she insists that the class must meet the certification requirements of Rule 23 of the Federal Rules of Civil Procedure, such as the existence of "questions of law or fact common to the class."[18] In a footnote, Barrett adds that the Administrative Procedure Act (APA) authorizes federal courts to vacate [annul] agency action, including presumably any agency rule that implements Trump's Order.[19] Third, Barrett agrees that injunctive relief for the parties of a case must constitute "complete relief," which may in some instances benefit nonparties, such as injunction against a noisy neighbor who blasts "loud music at all hours of the night." But she adds that such benefits are "incidental" only, without legal significance. Lastly, Barrett concedes that "complete relief" is more "complicated for state parties" because a universal injunction might be necessary to avoid the additional costs and administrative burdens of a "patchwork" system of citizenship. However, in response to these claims, Barrett observes that "complete relief" is not a "guarantee," but only "the maximum a court can provide." In addition, she notes that "complete relief" might be provided to the relevant state parties if district courts enjoined Trump's Order "within the respondent

---

ecourt.gov/opinions/24pdf/24a1063_6j37.pdf), quoting *Hilton v. Braunskill*, 481 U.S. 770, 776 (1987). However, in her dissent in *SSA v. AFSCME*, Justice Brown denied that the majority properly applied these four requirements for a stay to the facts of that case.

[17] *Trump v. CASA*, Justice Barrett's majority slip opinion, at 21.

[18] Rule 23. Class Actions, available at https://www.law.cornell.edu/rules/frcp/rule_23. Two weeks after the Supreme Court decided *Trump v. CASA*, a district judge in New Hampshire certified all children subject to Trump's Order as a class and enjoined its enforcement against any class member in *Barbara v. Trump*, available at https://www.courtlistener.com/docket/70651853/64/barbara-v-trump/.

[19] *Trump v. CASA*, Justice Barrett's majority opinion, FN 10 at 11.

States" or directed the Government to "treat covered [in-state] children as eligible for purposes of federally funded welfare benefits." In the end, Barrett declined to make a ruling on what remedy is necessary for the complete relief of the states, leaving the question to be resolved on a case-by-case basis in the lower courts. [20]

Three other justices address the issue of the availability of these alternative remedies in their concurring opinions. Regarding whether "complete relief" should ever benefit nonparties, Justice Thomas argues that it should do so "only when it would be 'all but impossible to devise relief that reaches only the plaintiffs.'"[21] Justice Alito remarks that district courts should not view the Court's "kibosh on universal injunctions ... as an invitation to certify nationwide classes without scrupulous adherence to the rigors of Rule 23."[22] In contrast, Justice Kavanaugh fully expects district courts to issue orders that are "the functional equivalent of a universal injunction," that such "nationally uniform answers" are at times appropriate prior to final judgment, and that the Supreme Court must be the ultimate decider.[23] At a minimum, the concurring opinions reveal differences among the justices regarding the suitability of remedies other than universal injunctions, an issue that will undoubtedly reappear in future cases.

Justice Sotomayor, who wrote the "principal" dissenting opinion, argues forcefully that the Court should deny Trump's request for a stay. First, she argues courts should automatically deny stays if an applicant is acting in "bad faith," indirectly hinting that Trump's Order may fall within this rule. Second, Trump has not established the requisite "irreparable harm" required for a stay because "it defies logic to say that maintaining a centuries-long status quo for a few months longer will irreparably injure the Government." In addition, an "irreparable harm" is not present because equity courts have provided relief to nonparties for "centuries" through "bills of peace"—a type of relief that evolved into injunctions against federal and state laws.[24] In her view, such injunctions are functionally

---

[20] *Id.* at 16, 17–19.

[21] *Trump v. CASA*, Justice Thomas's concurring slip opinion at 4.

[22] *Trump v. CASA*, Justice Alito's concurring slip opinion at 3–4.

[23] *Trump v. CASA*, Justice Kavanaugh's concurring slip opinion at 4–9.

[24] In her majority opinion, Justice Barrett denies that "bills of peace" are analogous to universal injunctions, claiming that, although they provided relief to nonparties, their use was confined to "limited circumstances" and provided relief, not universally, but rather to a "group [that] was small and cohesive." In her view, they were the predecessor of class action lawsuits, not universal injunctions. See her slip opinion at 12–14.

indistinguishable from universal injunctions. Accordingly, although the majority nods in the direction of equity's "flexibility," it in fact "ignores the very flexibility that historically allowed equity to secure complete justice," thereby improperly and unwisely "freezing in amber the precise remedies available at the time of the Judiciary Act [of 1789]." Lastly, Sotomayor insists, it is impossible to claim that a stay in this case serves the "public interest" because the Order "is patently unconstitutional." In effect, the "Court's decision is nothing less than an open invitation for the Government to bypass the Constitution" as well as undermine the "rule of law" and "democracy" itself.[25] Justice Brown, in her dissenting opinion, expands upon this theme. She voices her "deep disillusionment" with the Court's decision and claims that the majority's "legalese" regarding the equitable remedies of the High Court of Chancery is simply a "smokescreen." It is meant to hide the fact that the Court is permitting "the Executive to violate the Constitution with respect to anyone who has not yet sued," which is, in her view, "an existential threat to the rule of law."[26]

Constitutional Significance

Although formally a matter of statutory interpretation, *Trump v. CASA* is yet a major constitutional decision because it shifts power from the lower federal judiciary to the Executive Branch. The significance of the shift will depend on future Supreme Court decisions regarding lower-court class certifications under Rule 23(a), vacatur (or annulment) of agency rules under the APA, and injunctions that provide "complete relief" that have "incidental" benefits to nonparties. However, there is an irony here: in the very decision the Court prohibited lower-court universal injunctions, it issued one that ordered the Trump administration NOT to enforce the Citizenship Order for 30 days to give district judges an opportunity to consider the above alternative remedies. The Court has yet to explain how it is that the Judiciary Act of 1789 enabled it to issue such a universal injunction, but disabled lower federal courts from doing the same.

---

[25] *Trump v. CASA*, Justice Sotomayor's dissenting slip opinion at 14–15; 19–21, 24, 29, 39–40, 44.

[26] *Trump v. CASA*, Justice Brown's dissenting slip opinion at 2–3, 1.

CHAPTER 7

Wilcox v. Trump: The Death Rattle of the Independent Agency?

Jonathan David Shaub

In *Trump v. Wilcox*,[1] in an analysis consisting of just 401 words, the Supreme Court dramatically reshaped the federal government and significantly enhanced presidential power. The *Wilcox* opinion resolved two separate cases, each of which arose after President Trump purported to remove an official serving on the leadership board of a traditionally independent federal agency. On January 27, 2025, Trump informed Gwynne Wilcox that he was removing her from her position on the National Labor Relations Board (NLRB).[2] Similarly, on February 10, 2025, Trump purported to remove Cathy Harris from her position on the Merit Systems Protection Board (MSPB).[3] Both Wilcox and Harris had been confirmed

---

[1] 145 S. Ct. 1415, 1415 (2025).
[2] Wilcox v. Trump, 775 F. Supp. 3d 215, 222 (D.D.C. 2025).
[3] Harris v. Bessent, 775 F. Supp. 3d 164, 171 (D.D.C. 2025).

J. D. Shaub (✉)
University of Kentucky Rosenberg College of Law, Lexington, KY, USA
e-mail: Jonathan.shaub@uky.edu

© The Author(s), under exclusive license to Springer Nature Switzerland AG 2026
H. Schweber (ed.), *SCOTUS 2025*,
https://doi.org/10.1007/978-3-032-10231-7_7

by the Senate to terms of service that did not expire until 2028.[4] And, by statute, neither Wilcox nor Harris could be removed from her position without "cause"—that is, a showing of "malfeasance" or "neglect of duty," for example, that justified the removal.[5] Nevertheless, Trump claimed the authority to remove both Wilcox and Harris from their respective positions without any cause, arguing that the statutory restrictions on their removal violated his constitutional authority as President.

Both Wilcox and Harris sued to challenge Trump's purported removal, and lower courts—agreeing that the two officials were likely to win due to the statutory removal protection—reinstated them to their positions while the lawsuits continued.[6] The Department of Justice turned to the Supreme Court, however, asking the Court to step in on an expedited basis, stay the lower court decisions, and allow Trump to remove the two officials.[7] In its *Wilcox* decision, the Supreme Court obliged, blessing President Trump's removal of Wilcox and Harris from office. The Court resolved these cases rapidly through its emergency—or "shadow"—docket as opposed to the normal process of briefing and argument, and, as a result, the Court provided very limited reasoning for the result.[8] But that concision belies the import of the decision. The Court's decision in *Wilcox* appears to vitiate nearly a century of precedent. And it will have enormous ramifications for the structure of government going forward and for presidential control of administrative agencies, even those agencies Congress and past presidents have sought to insulate from political control. The Court did try in a few short words to minimize the impact of *Wilcox* on perhaps the most

---

[4] *Wilcox*, 777 F. Supp. 3d at 222; *Harris*, 777 F. Supp. 3d at 171.

[5] *See* 29 U.S.C. § 153(a) ("Any member of the Board may be removed by the President, upon notice and hearing, for neglect of duty or malfeasance in office, but for no other cause.") (NLRB); 5 U.S.C. § 1202(d) ("Any member may be removed by the President only for inefficiency, neglect of duty, or malfeasance in office.") (MSPB).

[6] *See* Harris v. Bessent, 2025 WL 1021435 (D.C. Cir. Apr. 7, 2025) (en banc) (per curiam).

[7] *See* Application to Stay the Judgments of the United States District Court for the District of Columbia and Request for Administrative Stay, *Trump v. Wilcox*, No. 24A966 (U.S.) (Apr. 9, 2025).

[8] *See* Steve Vladeck, *153. Living by the Ipse Dixit*, One First (May 26, 2025), https://www.stevevladeck.com/p/153-living-by-the-ipse-dixit?utm_source=publication-search (arguing, in relation to Wilcox, that "[t]he Court is doing too much through an unsigned and barely-explained order on the emergency docket"). For in-depth treatment of the Court's "shadow docket," see Stephen Vladeck, The Shadow Docket: How the Supreme Court Uses Stealth Rulings to Amass Power and Undermine the Republic (May 16, 2023).

important independent regulatory agency—the Federal Reserve—but it remains unclear whether that attempt will be successful.

The Question of the President's Removal Power

For nearly a century—beginning with its decision in *Humphrey's Executor v. United States* in 1935—the Supreme Court has interpreted the Constitution to allow for the creation of so-called "independent" agencies, agencies whose leadership cannot be removed by the President absent some showing of cause.[9] These agencies were designed to be expert bodies performing vital functions on behalf of the country, but removed from the whim of partisanship and the politics of any single party. Congress has created and past presidents signed into law a number of such entities over the last century, including, to name only a few, the Federal Trade Commission (FTC), the Securities and Exchange Commission (SEC), the NLRB, the MSPB, the independent counsel, and the Federal Reserve. *Humphrey's Executor* and its progeny have long stood for the principle that the Constitution does not mandate that the President have absolute removal power over the leaders of these independent entities because these agencies perform largely "quasi-legislative" or "quasi-judicial functions" and do not wield "substantial executive power."[10]

Harris and Wilcox argued that the NLRB and MSPB fell squarely within *Humphrey's Executor*'s purview as independent agencies controlled by a multimember boards that performed quasi-judicial functions and wielded minimal executive power.[11] Indeed, the prevailing consensus is that the NLRB and MSPB operate substantially similarly to the FTC.[12] The two officials also emphasized Congress's historical reliance on removal restrictions to ensure that expert agencies remained apolitical and

---

[9] 295 U.S. 602 (1935); *see generally* Kirti Datla & Richard L. Revesz, *Deconstructing Independent Agencies (and Executive Agencies)*, 98 Cornell L. Rev. 76 (2013) (describing the various attempts to create independence in administrative agencies).

[10] *Humphrey's Executor*, 295 U.S. at 629; *Seila Law LLC v. Consumer Financial Protection Bureau*, 591 U.S. 197, 216–18 (2020); *see also* Brief for Plaintiff-Appellee at 27–30, Wilcox v. Trump, No. 25-334 (U.S. App. D.C. Apr. 7, 2025) [hereinafter "Wilcox's Brief"].

[11] Wilcox's Brief, *supra* note 10, at 9–13; Plaintiff's Motion for Preliminary Injunction and Judgment on the Merits at 11, Harris v. Bessent, No. 1:25-cv-00412-RC.

[12] *See* Vladeck, *Living by the Ipse Dixit*, *supra* note 8.

independent, as well as the Court's repeated precedential statement that the President's removal power was "not absolute."[13]

In recent years, however, the Court has begun to express skepticism about independence within the executive branch, instead leaning toward a more "unitary" theory of the executive branch under the Constitution. In 1988, Justice Scalia wrote a dissenting opinion in *Morrison v. Olson* articulating this vision, suggesting that Article II of the Constitution vested all executive power in the President alone and that, therefore, the President must have control over all officers exercising such executive power.[14] All eight of the other Justices disagreed in *Morrison*. But in 2010 the Supreme Court adapted much of Justice Scalia's rationale in *Free Enterprise Fund v. Public Company Accounting Oversight Board*, concluding that statutory removal protections for an SEC accounting board were unconstitutional—the first time the Supreme Court had struck down statutory removal protections since *Humphrey's Executor*.[15]

More recently, in 2020, the Supreme Court went further, concluding in *Seila Law LLC v. Consumer Financial Protection Bureau* that the statutory removal protections for the single director of the Consumer Financial Protection Bureau (CFPB) were unconstitutional. In *Seila Law*, however, the Court distinguished and did not overrule *Humphrey's Executor*. Instead, the Court explained that, although the President generally had absolute authority to remove executive branch officials, *Humphrey's Executor* had recognized an exception to that authority for "multimember expert agencies that do not wield substantial executive power."[16] Because the CFPB at issue in *Seila Law* was not a "multimember" agency but headed by a single director, the *Seila* court explained, the CFPB was distinct from the FTC and thus the removal protections for the CFPB head were unconstitutional. The Supreme Court later applied *Seila* to strike down removal protections again in *Collins v. Yellen*—this time for the head of the Federal Housing Finance Agency (FHFA)—again determining that the single-headed nature of the agency distinguished it from the FTC in *Humphrey's Executor* and again concluding that the President must have unfettered removal power over sole agency heads.[17]

---

[13] Wilcox's Brief, *supra* note 10, at 19–22.
[14] *Morrison v. Olson*, 487 U.S. 654, 697–733 (1988) (Scalia, J., dissenting).
[15] 561 U.S. 477, 483–84 (2010).
[16] *Seila Law*, 591 U.S. at 218.
[17] 594 U.S. 220 (2021).

The arguments and outcome in *Wilcox* rested almost entirely on how broadly the Court would apply its decision in *Seila*, a determination largely dependent on the continuing vitality of *Humphrey's Executor*. In their briefs, Harris and Wilcox emphasized the Court's deliberate decision not to overrule or disturb the validity of *Humphrey's Executor* in *Seila* and *Collins*.[18] Additionally, Harris and Wilcox argued that both the NLRB and the MSPB are multimember expert agencies and not single-headed agencies like those at issue in *Seila* and *Collins*. The Trump administration, for its part, argued that *Humphrey's Executor* applied narrowly, only where an agency did not exercise *any* executive power, and asserted that both the NLRB and MSPB exercised such power.[19] The government pointed to the NLRB's power to grant remedies like "reinstatement," its "robust 'enforcement authority'," and its rulemaking authority in the realm of employer-employee relations as evidence that the board members "wield executive power" and thus must be removable at will.[20] The administration similarly highlighted the MSPB's enforcement authority, its power to review and invalidate rules and regulations issued by the Office of Personnel Management, and its ability to review the President's removal of inferior officers to conclude that President Trump could lawfully remove Harris.[21]

Most strikingly, however, the Trump administration sought to eliminate the precedential force of *Humphrey's Executor* entirely. It argued that the "assumption" in *Humphrey's Executor* that the FTC and other similar independent agencies did not exercise executive power "has since been 'repudiated' by the Supreme Court."[22] Consequently, in the administration's view, that foundational decision should "be understood as precedential only as to the specific question it resolved" and had little to no value for the current controversy.[23] In its view, because Article II of the Constitution vests *all* of the executive power in the President, the NLRB

---

[18] Wilcox's Brief, *supra* note 10, at 24; Merits Brief for Appellee at 18–23, Harris v. Bessent No. 25-5055 (U.S. App. D.C. Apr. 7, 2025) [hereinafter "Harris' Brief"].

[19] Brief for Appellant at 26–27, Harris v. Bessent & Wilcox v. Trump, Nos. 25-5036, 25-5055, 25-5057 (U.S. App. D.C. Mar. 27, 2025).

[20] *Id*. at 27–30 (citing *Seila Law*, 591 U.S. at 204).

[21] *Id*. at 33–37.

[22] *Id*. at 21 (quoting *Seila Law*, 591 U.S. at 239 (Thomas, J., concurring in part and dissenting in part)).

[23] *Id*. at 21.

and MSPB—and any other officer wielding any modicum of executive power—must be subject to the President's unfettered control.[24]

Wilcox, an Empowered President, and the Question of the Federal Reserve

Although the Trump administration prevailed in *Wilcox*, the precise rationale of the Court was anything but clear. The Court stated the general principle from *Seila* that "[b]ecause the Constitution vests the executive power in the President, he may remove without cause executive officers who exercise that power on his behalf, subject to narrow exceptions recognized by our precedents."[25] And it found that neither Wilcox nor Harris fit within those narrow exceptions because the administration could likely show that the NLRB and MSPB exercised "considerable executive power."[26] The Court did not explain, however, whether it now believed—contrary to the nearly century-old principle of *Humphrey's Executor*—that all agencies, including the FTC, exercised executive power and had to be directly answerable to the President *or* whether the Court believed there was something specific about the NLRB and MSPB that distinguished them from the FTC in *Humphrey's Executor*. Nor did it state specifically what authorities exercised by the NLRB and MSPB constituted "executive power."

Writing for three dissenters, Justice Kagan—like the district courts—disagreed and viewed *Wilcox* as a straightforward application of *Humphrey's Executor*. In her view, the structure and authorities of the NLRB and MSPB, both agencies exercising "quasi-judicial" functions and minimal executive power, closely resembles that of the FTC.[27] Indeed, if the NLRB and MSPB wield substantial executive power, then it is hard to conceive of an agency that does *not* wield such power and hard to see any continued applicability of *Humphrey's Executor*.[28]

---

[24] *Id.* at 2–3, 22, 26 ("Under [our view], any exercise of executive power subjects an agency head to the President's control.").

[25] *Trump v. Wilcox*, 145 S. Ct. 1415, 1415 (2025).

[26] *Id.*

[27] *Id.* at 1418 (Kagan, J., dissenting) ("Under [*Humphrey's Executor*], this case is easy, as the courts below found: The President has no legal right to relief.").

[28] *See* Wilcox Brief, *supra* note 10, at 30; *see also* Harris Brief, *supra* note 18, at 12 ("If the [MSPB]'s modest adjudicatory authority crosses the line ... there would be nothing left of *Humphrey's Executor*."); Vladeck, *Living by the Ipse Dixit*, *supra* note 8 ("[I]t would be very

One traditionally independent agency—the Federal Reserve—featured prominently in the arguments in *Wilcox*. There is perhaps no other agency whose expertise and independence are so intrinsic to its mission, and there is widespread agreement that the Federal Reserve and its decisions about monetary policy should not be subject to political whim or direct presidential control.[29] In their briefs, Wilcox and Harris repeatedly argued that if the Court declared the statutes prohibiting their removals without cause unconstitutional, the statutes protecting the members of the Board of Governors of the Federal Reserve and the Open Market Committee from removal without cause would also necessarily be unconstitutional. The Court went out of its way to address and reject this argument, taking time in the exceptionally brief decision to clarify that "[t]he Federal Reserve is a uniquely structured, quasi-private entity that follows in the distinct historical tradition of the First and Second Banks of the United States."[30] As Justice Kagan noted in her dissent and other commentators have pointed out, though, the Court provided no legal rationale for its "bespoke" exception for the Federal Reserve, an agency that likely exercises more "executive power" than the NLRB or MSPB.[31] And the Court's statement that the Federal Reserve follows the "tradition" of the First and Second Banks of the United States is highly suspect.[32]

The Court appears to have gone out of its way to calm financial markets by disclaiming the contention that the *Wilcox* decision would undermine the Federal Reserve's independence. But it did not provide any legal rationale for that reassurance, and the constitutional principles espoused by the Trump administration that the Court apparently found persuasive in *Wilcox* would appear to render that independence unconstitutional. One of the most important questions remaining after *Wilcox* is thus whether—and how—the Court will declare statutory removal protections

difficult for the Supreme Court to *strike down* the statutes requiring good cause to fire members of the NLRB and MSPB *without* overruling *Humphrey's Executor*[.]").

[29] *See, e.g.*, Steve Inskeep & Destinee Adams, *A Well-run Economy Needs an Independent Federal Reserve*, Says Former Reserve Bank Head, NPR (July 17, 2025, 12:25 PM), https://www.npr.org/2025/07/17/nx-s1-5469934/federal-reserve-trump-firing-independence.
[30] *Trump v. Wilcox*, 145 S. Ct. 1415, 1415 (2025).
[31] *See id.* at 1421 (Kagan, J., dissenting); Vladeck, *Living by the Ipse Dixit, supra* note 8.
[32] *See, e.g.*, Benjamin Dinovelli, *The Federal Reserve Exception*, Vanderbilt Law Research Paper (Jun. 3, 2025) (draft), available at https://papers.ssrn.com/sol3/papers.cfm?abstract_id=5277476; @Kexelchabot.bsky.social, Bluesky, https://bsky.app/profile/did:plc:6uefqyopaxhjvgv62quxlstr/post/3lpscpbxpns22?ref_src=embed (critiquing the Court's statement based on research into the founding-era Sinking Fund).

unconstitutional for every independent agency *except* the Federal Reserve or whether it will ultimately reject the Federal Reserve's independence as well.

Beyond the Federal Reserve, the immediate consequence of the *Wilcox* decision will be to enhance and extend the President's control over agencies and officials designed by Congress to be politically independent.[33] *Wilcox* significantly erodes the tradition of protecting some agencies from single-party, partisan control by allowing the President to threaten removal for disobedience or to simply remove all officials with whom he has policy disagreements.[34] On a more granular level, allowing President Trump to remove members of the MSPB—which itself adjudicates the legality of dismissals in the federal civil service—empowers the President to direct the Board's review of dismissals and implement a broad removal policy even with respect to the career civil service.[35] In sum, nonpartisan agencies that previously exercised some measure of independence will now be under the thumb of the President—a partisan official. Indeed, two months after *Wilcox*, the Court issued a two-paragraph order in another case on its emergency docket, upholding Trump's removal of a member of the Consumer Product Safety Commission (CPSC)—another formerly independent agency—without cause.[36] In that case, the district court had acknowledged the result in *Wilcox*, but it had considered itself still bound by *Humphrey's Executor*, which had not been overruled or narrowed given that *Wilcox* was an emergency order. The Supreme Court chastised the district court for not following *Wilcox*, emphasizing that although the Supreme Court's "interim orders are not conclusive as to the merits, they inform how a court should exercise its equitable discretion in like case."[37] Because the CPSC "exercises executive power in the same manner as the NLRB," the Court blessed Trump's removal of another formerly independent official.[38]

---

[33] Bob Bauer & Jack Goldsmith, *The Supreme Court's Important Decision on Presidential Removal*, Exec. Functions (May 23, 2025), https://executivefunctions.substack.com/p/the-supreme-courts-important-decision?utm_source=publication-search.

[34] *Id.*

[35] *Id.*

[36] Trump v. Boyle, No. 25A11 (July 23, 2025), available at https://www.supremecourt.gov/opinions/24pdf/25a11_2cp3.pdf.

[37] *Id.*

[38] *Id.*

Numerous other cases and controversies regarding President Trump's removal of executive branch officials are also percolating, including his purported removal of an FTC Commissioner in a direct challenge to *Humphrey's Executor*.[39] The Trump administration has aggressively pursued a maximalist view of presidential power and adopted wholesale the unitary executive theory,[40] claiming constitutional authority to fire numerous officials that Congress and past presidents sought to protect from control by the political party in power. Trump has removed career employees in the civil service, an institution that grew out of a desire to hire and fire government employees based on merit and expertise as opposed to political party.[41] He has removed officials who have traditionally been insulated from such political pressures, including the statistician responsible for accurate job data.[42] And he has even purported to remove officials working in largely *legislative* capacities pursuant to this claimed constitutional power.[43]

The *Wilcox* opinion suggests the Supreme Court shares this vision of robust presidential power. And it enables future Presidents to reshape broad swaths of the federal government according to political and personal preference. As Justice Kagan put it, dissenting from the Court's order in the later CPSC case, "[b]y allowing the President to remove [officials] for no reason other than their party affiliation," the Court is now allowing the President to "negate[ ] Congress's choice of agency bipartisanship and independence," and to do so across the entirety federal

[39] *See* Slaughter v. Trump, No. 25-909 (LLA), 2025 WL 1984396 (D.D.C. July 17, 2025) (initial district court ruling on the validity of Trump's purported removal of Rebecca Kelly Slaughter, an FTC Commissioner).

[40] *See* Jack Goldsmith, *Maximum Executive Power and the Fate of the Unitary Executive*, Exec. Functions (Jan. 28, 2025), https://executivefunctions.substack.com/p/maximum-executive-power-and-the-fate.

[41] *See* Eric Katz, "Trump admin tells judge it can fire at least some career feds at any time for any reason," *Gov't Exec.* (July 17, 2025), https://www.govexec.com/management/2025/07/trump-admin-tells-judge-it-can-fire-least-some-career-feds-any-time-any-reason/406797/; *see also* 5 U.S.C. § 2301 (setting forth the principles of a merit-based civil service system).

[42] *See* Ashley Ahn, "She was an economist with bipartisan support. Then Trump fired her." *N.Y. Times* (Aug. 2, 2025 5:31 PM ET), https://www.nytimes.com/2025/08/02/us/politics/until-trump-fired-her-she-was-an-economist-with-bipartisan-support.html?smid=url-share.

[43] *See* Assoc. Press, "President Trump fires Librarian of Congress Carla Hayden," NPR (May 9, 2025 1:18 AM ET), https://www.npr.org/2025/05/09/g-s1-65271/librarian-of-congress-fired.

government.[44] The district courts in both the *Harris* and *Wilcox* cases made similar points, highlighting the "150-year history of independent, multimember commissions" that the Trump administration's arguments threatened.[45] The Court's decision in *Wilcox* made that threat a reality.

Wilcox is not the last word on the question of the President's power of removal. The Court will eventually have to explain its theory of presidential power in full, either in the *Wilcox* case itself on further consideration or in a future case. But unless the Court changes course, the *Wilcox* decision suggests that the country's over a century-old experiment of utilizing expert, independent agencies and officials to perform tasks not subject to the President's political direction may be at an end.

---

[44] Trump v. Boyle, No. 25A11 (July 23, 2025) (Kagan, J., dissenting), available at https://www.supremecourt.gov/opinions/24pdf/25a11_2cp3.pdf.

[45] *Wilcox v. Trump*, 775 F. Supp. 3d at 223–24; *see also Harris*, 775 F. Supp. 3d at 175–78.

CHAPTER 8

Federal Communications Commission v. Consumer's Research: Applying the Nondelegation Doctrine to Agency Discretion over Tax and Fee Obligations

Bernard W. Bell

Federal Communications Commission v. Consumer Research[1] involved a seemingly esoteric question: Does authorizing the Federal Communications Commission (the FCC) to determine the rates telecommunications providers must pay to support projects relating to ensuring universal telecommunications service violate the nondelegation doctrine? But the case brought together several divergent strands of administrative law.

The Constitution delegates to Congress *all* legislative powers granted under it. From this flows the nondelegation doctrine—Congress cannot delegate its legislative powers to other branches of government or private entities. The doctrine's rationale is simply stated. To maintain

---

[1] Dkt. No. 24–354, slip op., 606 U. S. ____, 145 S.Ct. 2482 (June 27, 2025).

B. W. Bell (✉)
Rutgers Law School, Newark, NJ, USA
e-mail: bbell@law.rutgers.edu

accountability in a democratic government, Congress must make its own decisions about regulatory obligations.[2] However, the Supreme Court long ago held that so long as Congress legislated an "intelligible principle" to follow, it could allow the President or executive branch agencies to "fill in the details."[3]

With respect to private parties, the nondelegation doctrine is seemingly more absolute; Congress cannot delegate legislative power to private entities.[4] But here too there is nuance; an agency may enlist such entities to provide "assistance" in making regulatory decisions.[5]

The nondelegation doctrine has garnered considerable judicial and academic attention, especially in comparison to the paucity of cases in which it has been successfully invoked. Some scholars and judges have advocated the doctrine's revitalization.[6] More modestly, others have suggested declaring some legislative functions nondelegable, such as the power to tax.[7] Nondelegation doctrine concerns have had a greater impact upon statutory interpretation. Both the "major questions doctrine," limiting agencies' ability to resolve certain statutory ambiguities,[8] and plain statement interpretive canons, requiring that Congress speak clearly when breaching certain principles, reflect an effort to ensure that Congress makes critical policy decisions.[9]

At the same time, the accountability of independent agencies has been a core debate in administrative law. In the Supreme Court, and to a certain extent among scholars, the debate has focused on the President's power to appoint and remove agency officials. But concern has also been expressed regarding the financial independence some of these agencies enjoy due to

---

[2] John Hart Ely, Democracy and Distrust: A Theory of Judicial Review 131–34 (1981); Gundy v. U.S., 588 U.S. 128, 154–57 (2019) (Gorsuch, J. dissenting).

[3] J. W. Hampton, Jr., & Co. v. United States, 276 U.S. 394, 409 (1928).

[4] A.L.A. Schechter Poultry Corp. v. U.S., 295 U.S. 495, 537 (1935); Carter v. Carter Coal Co., 298 U.S. 238, 311 (1936).

[5] Sunshine Anthracite Coal Co. v. Adkins, 310 U.S. 381, 388, 399 (1940).

[6] David Schoenbrod, Power Without Responsibility: How Congress Abuses the People Through Delegation (Yale Univ. Press, 1993); Gundy v. U.S., 588 U.S. 128, 154–57 (Gorsuch, J. dissenting).

[7] *E.g.*, James R. Hines & Kyle D. Logue, *Delegating Tax*, 114 Mich. L. Rev. 235, 239 (2015).

[8] West Virginia v. EPA, 597 U.S. 697 (2022).

[9] See, e.g., Cass R. Sunstein, *Nondelegation Canons*, 67 U. Chi. L. Rev. 315, 322 (2000).

funding streams separate and apart from the annual congressional appropriations process.[10]

The Statutory/Regulatory Framework

Widespread access to telecommunications benefits all subscribers given telecommunications systems' "network effects."[11] The Communications Act of 1934 required that the FCC employ its powers to set "just and reasonable" telecommunication rates in ways that cross-subsidized those groups least likely to be offered service on a purely market basis. That cross-subsidization was implicit. Rates were set such that long-distance service subsidized local service, business users subsidized residential users, and urban subscribers subsidized rural ones.[12]

Deregulation came to federal telecommunications regulation with the passage of the Telecommunications Act of 1996.[13] With regard to ensuring universal service, the Act mandated that the FCC transform its regulatory regime from an implicit one, using ratemaking, to an explicit one, employing subsidies. The focus of the subsidy regime would be a new universal service fund. Every interstate telecommunications carrier was to contribute to the fund, which would "pay for subsidy programs for designated populations and facilities needing improved [telecommunications] access."[14]

Congress set forth six principles on which the FCC is to base its policies. First, "[q]uality services should be available at just, reasonable, and affordable rates." Second, "[a]ccess to advanced telecommunications and information services should be provided in all regions." Third, low-income consumers and those in rural, insular, and high-cost areas should have access to services "reasonably comparable to those services provided in urban areas … [at] reasonably comparable to rates." Fourth, all telecommunications providers "should make an equitable and nondiscriminatory contribution" to ensuring universal service. Fifth, the mechanisms "to

---

[10] Consumer Financial Protection Bureau v. Community Finan. Servs. Ass'n, 601 U.S. 416 (2024).

[11] Michael L. Katz and Carl Shapiro, *Systems Competition and Network Effects*, 8 J. Econ. Perspectives 93, 94, 96–97 (1994)("network effects" occur when "the value of membership to one user is positively affected" when the network is enlarged).

[12] *Consumers Research*, slip op. at 3–4; id. at 3 (Gorsuch, J. dissenting).

[13] Pub. L. 104-104, 110 STAT. 58 (Feb. 8, 1996).

[14] 47 U.S.C. §254(a), (d); *Consumers Research*, slip op. at 4.

preserve and advance universal service" must be "specific, predictable and sufficient." And sixth, "[e]lementary and secondary schools and classrooms, health care providers, and libraries should have access to certain advanced telecommunications services." Section 254(b) also gave the FCC the power to supplement this list with "[s]uch other principles as ... the Commission determine[s] are necessary and appropriate for the protection of the public interest, convenience, and necessity and are consistent with this chapter."[15]

In deciding upon the services the universal service fund would support, the FCC was directed to "consider" four criteria. First, it has to assess how essential the service is to education, public health, or public safety. Second, it has to consider the extent to which the service "through the operation of market choices by customers, [had] been subscribed to by a substantial majority of residential customers." Third, the Commission must consider the level of telecommunications carriers' deployment of the service. Fourth, the Commission must assess the extent to which including such services in the universal service program is "consistent with the public interest, convenience, and necessity."[16]

Contributions to the universal service fund are made on a quarterly basis; determining the amounts owed involves establishing the "contribution factor" used to determine each carrier's obligations.[17] The process of calculating the contribution factor begins with the Universal Service Administrative Company (USAC), a non-profit corporation owned by an association of telecommunications carriers. In 1998, the FCC appointed USAC as the Fund's "permanent Administrator" to manage the Fund's day-to-day operations.[18]

THE FIFTH CIRCUIT'S RULING

Consumers' Research mounted several challenges to the universal service fund regime in various courts of appeal. Its first two efforts failed, as the Sixth and Eleventh Circuits rejected Consumers' Research's nondelegation doctrine challenges.[19] But the third time would be the charm—the

---

[15] 47 U.S.C. §254.
[16] 47 U.S.C. §254(c)(1)(A)-(D).
[17] *Consumers' Research*, slip op. at 7.
[18] Id. (citing 47 CFR §54.701(a)).
[19] Consumers' Research v. FCC, 67 F.4th at 773 (6th Cir. 2023); Consumers' Research v. FCC, 88 F.4th 917, 921 (11th Cir. 2023), *cert. denied*, 144 S. Ct. 2629 (2024).

Fifth Circuit, sitting *en banc*, found the universal service regime unconstitutional.[20]

In upholding the nondelegation doctrine challenge, the Fifth Circuit acknowledged the "intelligible principle" test. In its view, however, section 254 failed that test. The provision was merely "a hollow shell that Congress created for FCC to fill" – "so amorphous that no reviewing court could ever possibly invalidate any FCC action taken in its name." [21] The Court found the extraordinary breadth of section 254's delegation "especially troubling" because it granted the FCC the power to raise revenues to fund the program. Thus, section 254 essentially nullifies Congress' appropriations power, insulating the FCC from Congress' "principal tool" to control the FCC's universal service decisions. The FCC was likewise insulated from presidential control, because of the Commissioner's tenure protections.[22]

In addition, the Fifth Circuit found that FCC's sub-delegation of authority to USAC had two private nondelegation doctrine infirmities. First it failed to satisfy the test for permissible agency use of private entities for assistance. Second, Congress had not expressly authorized such a subdelegation.

The Fifth Circuit found it unnecessary to rule on either the public or private nondelegation grounds standing alone. Instead, it asserted that two or more aspects of a regulatory regime that are not themselves unconstitutional can violate separation of powers principles when combined. Engaging in a "holistic" separation of powers assessment, the court held that "the combination of Congress's sweeping delegation to FCC and FCC's unauthorized subdelegation" to USAC doomed section 254. Such "double-layered delegation," lacks support "in history or tradition" and "undermine[s] democratic accountability."[23]

---

[20] Consumers' Research v. Federal Communications Commission, 109 F.4th 743 (5th Cir. 2024)(en banc).
[21] Id. at 760.
[22] Id. at 762–63.
[23] Id., at 782–84.

The Supreme Court Opinions

The Opinion of the Court

Writing for the majority, Justice Kagan reaffirmed the "intelligible principle" standard for testing congressional delegations to agencies in an opinion joined by Justices Roberts, Sotomayor, Kavanaugh, Barrett, and Jackson. Kagan acknowledged that the breadth of permissible delegation "varies according to the scope of the power congressionally conferred." Nevertheless, the Court had almost always upheld delegations when Congress has (1) made clear "'the general policy' the agency must pursue and 'the boundaries of [the agency's] delegated authority,' and (2) provided sufficient standards to enable 'the courts and the public [to] ascertain whether the agency' has followed the law."[24]

The majority refused to apply a special nondelegation rule applied to tax statutes, rejecting Consumers' Research's, and the dissenters', argument that Congress must set a "definite" or "objective limit" on how much money an agency can collect," that is, "a numeric cap, a fixed rate, or the equivalent." Kagan cited *J. W. Hampton & Co. v. United States*, and *Skinner v. Mid-America Pipeline Co.*, as precedents rejecting that proposition.[25] Indeed, in *Skinner* the Court had explained that "nothing" in the Constitution's text, structure, or history "distinguish[es] Congress' power to tax from its other enumerated powers" in terms of delegation of "authority to the Executive." Moreover, Consumers' Research's proposed test would throw into doubt a host of statutes Congress had enacted based on the Court's nondelegation doctrine precedents.[26]

Moreover, a numerically limited revenue-raising statute can "leave[ ] an agency with boundless power," such as a statute authorizing the FCC to assess up to $5 trillion in universal service fees. Such a statute would not vindicate the nondelegation doctrine's purpose, namely constraining the "degree of policy judgment" left to agencies. By contrast, a provision imposing qualitative constraints upon an agency, like section 254's requirement of "sufficient" funds, might well do so more effectively.[27]

---

[24] *Consumers' Research*, slip op. at 11.
[25] Consumers' Research at 12–13; see, *J. W. Hampton & Co. v. United States*, 276 U.S. 394, 409 (1928); *Skinner v. Mid-America Pipeline Co.*, 490 U.S. 212, 220 (1989).
[26] *Consumers' Research*, slip op. at 13–14.
[27] *Consumers' Research*, slip op. at 18–19.

The Court rejected claims that the statute's criteria left the FCC unbounded discretion. In context, section 254(b)'s provision that services "should," rather than "shall," be made available at "reasonable[] and affordable rates," *required* the FCC to ensure the reasonableness and affordability of rates for universal services. The FCC had no power to require services that could not be delivered affordably.[28] Each of section 254(c)'s four principles that the agency was required to "consider" had to be satisfied; none could be disregarded because the other principles had been met.[29]

The Court accused Consumers' Research of reading Section 254 "extravagantly" to enhance its constitutional challenge, an approach that departed from the Court's practice of reading statutes to comport with the Constitution when it is possible to do so.[30]

The Court then turned to the "private" nondelegation doctrine to assess the role the FCC had given USAC. An agency may enlist private parties to provide recommendations so long as the agency retains decision-making power. Here, the FCC had done so. The Commission appoints the USAC's Board of Directors and approves its budget. It explicitly precludes USAC from making "policy," directs USAC to carry out its tasks "consistent with" the FCC's dictates, and subjects its actions to *de novo* Commission review.[31]

Finally, the Court turned to the Fifth Circuit's "combination theory—that a constitutional non-violation plus a second constitutional non-violation may equal a constitutional violation." The problem, said Kagan, was that the layers of questionable delegations on which the Fifth Circuit focused operate on different axes. The *Hampton* "intelligible principle" doctrine limits Congress's power to delegate legislative power to agencies; the private nondelegation doctrine limits the power of a governmental entity to confer its authority upon private entities. Thus, a meritless public nondelegation challenge plus a meritless private nondelegation challenge cannot be combined to make a meritorious "combination" claim.[32]

---

[28] Id., at 26–27.
[29] Id., at 27.
[30] Id. at 29–30.
[31] Id. at 30–32.
[32] Id. at 34–37.

The Dissent

Writing for the dissenters, Justice Gorsuch focused only on the "public" nondelegation doctrine challenge. Gorsuch characterized section 254 as a congressional directive requiring the FCC to "decide for itself what the concept [of universal service] meant, to fund programs consistent with [agency's] understanding of that concept, and then to tax telecommunications carriers to pay for such programs."[33]

In terms of what services qualified for designation as universal services, the dissenters did not find the section 254(b) and 254(c) factors confining. They were a "mash of four factors and six principles" that the FCC is left to balance "against one another when they conflict." They disagreed with the majority's reading that all four 254(b) criteria had to be met, concluding that each of the criteria need only be "considered."[34]

Asserting that the universal service fee is a "tax," Gorsuch argued that "[t]axation ranks among the government's greatest powers," and its most potentially destructive. From precedent, he derived the following rule: in any statute delegating the power to tax domestically, Congress must prescribe the tax rate. Gorsuch acknowledged that Congress has sometimes declined to supply a rate and instead opted to cap the total sum the Executive may collect. However, he noted section 254 even lacked that.[35]

Gorsuch was unimpressed by the majority's conclusion that the qualitative limits on the power to assess a "tax" served as an adequate alternative for a set tax rate or cap. The statutory command that the FCC should raise funds "sufficient" to "preserve and advance universal service" was insufficient. First, section 254 does not precisely define "universal service" and the phrase lacks any established meaning. The four criteria for determining the "evolving" standard of universal service, he said, are no more than a "preface of generalities as to permissible aims."[36] Likewise, he claimed that the principles set forth in subsection (b) are inadequate—each is framed as a "should," not a "must," and could thus be ignored by the FCC in service of the others.[37]

Responding to the majority's point that a statutory cap could confer far more discretion than a qualitative limitation on the amount of an exaction,

---

[33] *Consumers Research, supra*, slip op. at 5 (Gorsuch, J., dissenting).
[34] Id. at 5–7 (Gorsuch, J., dissenting).
[35] Id. at 14–16 (Gorsuch, J., dissenting).
[36] Id. at 18–19 (Gorsuch, J., dissenting) (quoting *Schechter Poultry, supra*, 295 U.S. at 537).
[37] Id. at 20–21 (Gorsuch, J., dissenting).

Gorsuch explained that even if Congress authorized a ludicrously high cap the requirement would enhance accountability—Congress's responsibility for the potential tax level would be clear.

Conclusion

Given the Supreme Court's nondelegation precedents, section 254 would seem a poor candidate for a nondelegation doctrine challenge. The directions Congress included in section 254 seem more detailed than those in many statutory provisions the Court has previously upheld. The section 254 considerations do not yield determinate answers, but the Court has already held that the "intelligible principle" need not produce determinate answers. In any event, section 254's level of detail hardly suggests a complete congressional abdicated of responsibility.

The Fifth Circuit teed up this case for the Court to modify the delegation doctrine in important ways, and the case could have marked a significant break from almost a century of precedents. The Court could have begun to cabin the nondelegation doctrine with respect to agencies' powers to raise revenue. More radically, the Court could have used the case to jettison the "intelligible principle" approach altogether.

Instead, a solid majority of the Court appears to have rejected both paths, making the decision somewhat anticlimactic. Six Justices seem comfortable with, or at least resigned to, the continued relative quiescence of the nondelegation doctrine, viewing most delegations of policy-making authority to executive agencies as constitutional.

Nevertheless, we can expect Justice Gorsuch, as well as Justices Thomas and Alito, to continue their efforts to convince their colleagues that a more robust approach to the nondelegation doctrine is possible. But also expect the Court to continue to pursue approaches like the major questions doctrine that can vindicate, by other means, the values the nondelegation doctrine is designed to serve.

CHAPTER 9

Barnes v. Felix on Excessive Force Claims Against Police

Jasmine Farrier

In *Barnes v. Felix*,[1] the Supreme Court ruled unanimously in favor of the "totality of circumstances" legal approach to evaluating claims of excessive force by local police. This decision vacated and remanded the Fifth Circuit Court of Appeal's use of "moment-of-the-threat," a narrower window of time when reviewing police officers' decisions to use force. These two approaches differ on the time snapshot and relevant information needed to assess the reasonableness of an officer's action. The "moment of threat" looks at the instant, from the officer's perspective, that led to their use of force. The "totality of circumstances" perspective expands the time horizon under review to encompass a range of preceding actions and events leading up to the officer's decision to use force to counter a perceived threat. The Supreme Court's embrace of a broader chronology for

---

[1] *Barnes v. Felix*, 605 U.S. 73 (2025).

J. Farrier (✉)
University of Louisville, Louisville, KY, USA
e-mail: J.farrier@louisville.edu

© The Author(s), under exclusive license to Springer Nature Switzerland AG 2026
H. Schweber (ed.), *SCOTUS 2025*,
https://doi.org/10.1007/978-3-032-10231-7_9

assessing legal challenges removed a long-standing circuit split on the issue but sidestepped more controversial consideration of whether the police officer's own actions may have contributed to this traffic stop's escalation.

This case began with a local public safety official's traffic stop and attempted car search. The relevant constitutional question concerns the Fourth Amendment's standards and precedents surrounding reasonable searches. The Supreme Court's opinion said that a full legal evaluation required careful examination of actions by both parties before and during the traffic stop that led to the officer's decision to shoot, in this case resulting in the driver's death. While a police officer's own actions can be relevant under the "totality" standard, the Justices declined to engage the issue in this case.

In addition to the Fifth Circuit, the Second, Fourth, and Eighth Circuits had also utilized the now-rejected moment-of-the-threat approach. Supreme Court scholars have long analyzed how circuit splits influence which cases make the annual merits docket. Many of those splits concern long-standing ideological legal divisions.[2] In this case, the circuit split did not presage an ideologically divided Supreme Court decision. The unanimous ruling showed the justices' narrow common ground on using the totality standard without dictating what and whose preceding actions lower courts should take into account in this or other cases.

Background of Case

Roberto Felix Jr. was a Deputy Constable with the Harris County Constable Precinct Five near Houston, Texas. On April 28, 2016, around 2:40pm, Felix received a radio alert about a Toyota Corolla on the highway with outstanding toll violations. Felix saw the Corolla, turned on his patrol car's lights, and initiated a traffic stop. Twenty-four-year-old Ashtian Barnes pulled over to the left shoulder. Felix approached on the driver's side door and requested license and proof of insurance. Barnes replied he did not have his license and the car was his girlfriend's rental. Felix commented that he smelled marijuana and asked Barnes if there was anything else Felix should know. Felix also asked Barnes more than once to

---

[2] See, for example, Deborah Beim and Kelly Rader, "Setting the Supreme Court's Policy Agenda," *Journal of Law and Courts* 12 (2): 239–58 (2024), https://doi.org/10.1017/jlc.2024.5.

stop "digging around" through papers during their interaction. Barnes indicated that he may have identification in the trunk. Felix asked Barnes to pop the trunk from inside the car. Barnes did so and turned off the car. This first part of the stop lasted under two minutes.

Next, Officer Felix placed his right hand on his gun holster and asked Mr. Barnes to exit the car. Barnes opened the door but did not exit. Instead, Barnes turned the car back on. Felix unholstered his gun and, as the car began to move forward, jumped on the doorsill. Felix yelled twice "don't fucking move." With his head above the car, after about two seconds after getting on the doorsill, Felix fired two shots inside the car. While hit, Barnes stopped the car and put it in park. This part of the stop lasted about an additional three seconds. Felix made a radio call for backup, and by the time additional officers arrived, around 2:57pm, Barnes was found dead in the car.[3]

Janice Barnes filed a civil suit against Deputy Constable Felix for excessive force on behalf of her son. She alleged Felix deprived her son of constitutional rights under federal law and the Fourth Amendment. US civil rights laws allow a person to sue local and state officials for alleged violations of federal statute and/or constitutional rights.[4]

The district court granted summary judgment to Felix, saying that Ms. Barnes had not met the burden to show Felix's actions were "objectively unreasonable." Citing precedent, the district court concentrated only on the two seconds that included Felix's jumping on the car's doorsill and firing the first shot inside the car as Mr. Barnes began to drive away. At that moment, the district court concluded, Felix could reasonably think that he was at risk of serious harm.[5]

The Fifth Circuit Court of Appeals confirmed the district court's ruling. The appellate court concluded that Deputy Constable Felix could have reasonably concluded his own life was in danger and therefore did not violate Mr. Barnes's constitutional and statutory rights.[6] Notably, Appellate Senior Judge Patrick Higginbotham wrote the three-judge opinion as well as a separate concurrence, saying, "the moment of threat doctrine starves the reasonableness analysis by ignoring relevant facts to the expense of life." Higginbotham added that "a routine traffic stop has

---

[3] *Barnes v. Felix*, 605 U.S. 73 (2025), pages 1–2.
[4] 42 U. S. C. §1983.
[5] 532 F. Supp. 3d 463 (SD Tex. 2021), pages 468–472.
[6] 91 F. 4th (5th Cir. 2024), pages 393–394 and 397–398.

again ended in the death of an unarmed black man," and urged the Supreme Court to resolve the circuit split, noting four circuits used moment of threat and eight used totality of circumstances standards.[7]

Consensus at Oral Argument

The constitutional question before the US Supreme Court was "whether and to what extent circumstances leading up to an officer's use of force are relevant to determining whether that use of force was reasonable under the Fourth Amendment."[8]

Nathaniel A.G. Zelinsky represented Janice Barnes individually and on behalf of Ashtian Barnes's estate. In oral argument on January 22, 2025, Mr. Zelinsky opened by invoking Justice Scalia in a different traffic stop case, saying that the Court must "slosh through the fact-bound morass of reasonableness."[9]

Mr. Zelinsky described the lower courts' use of the "moment of threat" standard as a "legal amnesia [that] is incompatible with precedent, conflicts with common law, and defies common sense."[10] In response to a question from Justice Thomas on how many seconds would be relevant other than the two when Deputy Constable Felix jumped on the car, Zelinsky said, "if you include an extra three seconds, then you would look at the seizure in its totality."[11]

Justice Kavanaugh asked what Felix, or any officer of the law, should do if a car starts to drive off from a traffic stop. Mr. Zelinsky said in many circumstances, there are four other options: tracking via cameras on the highway, radioing other officers, following, and license plate tracking. Zelinsky added: "we're not suggesting that somebody should just get away scot-free, but it is unreasonable to use deadly force because what happened was Officer Felix put himself in a position where he had no alternative but to shoot the driver."[12] Later in the oral argument, Justice Kavanaugh returned to this question and asked when it would be appro-

---

[7] Ibid., pages 398 and 400–401.

[8] Elizabeth B. Prelogar et al., *On Writ of Certiorari to the United States Court of Appeals for the Fifth Circuit, Brief for the United States as Amicus Curiae Supporting Vacatur and Remand*, 1, https://www.justice.gov/d9/2025-02/12-1239_barnes.pdf.

[9] *Scott v. Harris*, 550 U.S. 372 (2007), page 383.

[10] *Barnes v. Felix* oral arguments transcript, 22 January 2024, page 1.

[11] Ibid., page 2.

[12] Ibid., page 3.

priate for an officer to jump on a car as it pulled away. Mr. Zelinsky replied that while there are some scenarios that could justify jumping on or in front of a car, shooting a driver while the car is moving could endanger others.[13]

Justice Alito asked, in effect, if it was necessary to assess the reasonableness of Officer Felix's own actions to jump on the car for courts to assess whether this outcome constituted an unreasonable search. Zelinsky replied that "we'd be happy with a very narrow holding," meaning that it was not necessary to examine in detail whether Officer Felix's actions directly contributed to his own fear for his life.[14]

Zoe Jacoby represented the United States and opened by agreeing with Mr. Zelinsky that the moment of threat standard was not correct. "The Fifth Circuit analyzed this case by examining only the so-called moment of the threat and categorically ignoring all prior events. None of the parties defends that approach ... and the Court probably doesn't need to go further and delineate the precise bounds of when force will be sort of reasonable or not."[15] Justice Jackson asked whether there is confusion or concern between the eight circuits that use the totality of circumstances standard. Jacoby answered, "not to my knowledge ... I'm not aware of a problem in the circuits that are correctly applying a totality-of-the-circumstances approach ... we're really just interested in correcting the Fifth Circuit's legal error ... we have no position on the facts of this case."[16]

Charles McCloud represented Deputy Constable Felix and opened his argument by rejecting the concept of officer-created danger theories, prompting several justices to remind him that the lower court would deal with that question and it was not the focus of the appeal. In a colloquy with Justice Gorsuch, McCloud repeated that his client wants "an objective inquiry that looks at the totality of the circumstances to determine whether the officer genuinely believed there was a threat."[17] McCloud's use of "genuinely believed" emphasized the subjective view of the officer, rather than the more objective "reasonably believed" phrasing more common in the totality standard.

---

[13] Ibid., pages 9, 10, 12.
[14] Ibid., pages 5 and 19.
[15] Ibid., pages 15 and 16.
[16] Ibid., pages 26, 27.
[17] Ibid., pages 31, 32, 34.

Court's Holding and Concurrence

The Supreme Court held unanimously that a Fourth Amendment claim of excessive force against a law enforcement officer requires an assessment of reasonableness that must include totality of the circumstances. While any number of facts may or may not be relevant, "no rule that precludes consideration of prior events in assessing a police shooting is reconcilable with the fact-dependent and context-sensitive approach we have prescribed. A court deciding a use-of-force case cannot review the totality of the circumstances if it has put on chronological blinders."[18]

Although Justice Kagan's opinion noted that the moment-of-threat standard is too narrow, and a court must "consider all the relevant circumstances, including facts and events leading up to the climactic moment," the Court did not address "whether or how an officer's own 'creation of a dangerous situation' factors into the reasonableness analysis. The courts below never confronted that issue, and it was not the basis of the petition for certiorari." [19]

Justice Kagan also explained that the totality standard did not inherently or automatically favor one side or the other regarding excessive-force claims: "Taking account of that context may benefit either party.... Prior events may show, for example, why a reasonable officer would have perceived otherwise ambiguous conduct of a suspect as threatening. Or instead they may show why such an officer would have perceived the same conduct as innocuous. The history of the interaction, as well as other past circumstances known to the officer, thus may inform the reasonableness of the use of force."[20]

Justice Kavanaugh wrote a concurrence, joined by Justices Thomas, Alito, and Barrett. "I join the Court's opinion. I agree that the officer's actions during the traffic stop in this case should be assessed based on the totality of the circumstances. I write separately to add a few points about the dangers of traffic stops for police officers, particularly when as here the driver pulls away in the midst of the stop."[21]

While acknowledging that most traffic stops do not escalate, the concurrence included a detailed summary of prior cases and incidents where traffic stops turned deadly, with police officers as victims. Kavanaugh also

---

[18] *Barnes* decision, page 7.
[19] Ibid., page 9.
[20] Ibid., page 6.
[21] *Barnes*, Kavanaugh concurrence at 1.

noted that traffic stops for expired registrations, missing license plates, and stolen vehicle alerts led to police officers' apprehending such prominent defendants as Oklahoma City bomber Timothy McVeigh and serial killer Ted Bundy.[22] Citing possible offenses as varied as drug possession, kidnapping, immigration violations, and even potentially using the car itself in a terrorist attack, "fleeing from the traffic stop could suggest that the driver is preparing to commit or has committed a more serious crime—and is attempting to evade detection or arrest."[23]

While explaining there are "no easy or risk-free answers," Kavanaugh listed a variety of options for police officers to consider in the split-second decision moment if a driver pulls away abruptly during a stop. "In analyzing the reasonableness of an officer's conduct at a traffic stop, particularly traffic stops where the driver has suddenly pulled away, courts must appreciate the extraordinary dangers and risks facing police officers and the community at large."[24]

The totality standard emphasizes "reasonableness" through the perspective of a hypothetical officer in a similar situation rather than through the benefit of hindsight in a particular situation. Both the decision and concurrence emphasized the need to include more information and context but purposefully avoided defining precisely how this standard would be applied in this or other similar cases.

CONCLUSIONS AND FUTURE IMPLICATIONS

Beginning in 2015, the FBI began to track police-involved "use of force" incidents. These data "offers big-picture insights, rather than information on specific incidents. The collection does not assess or report whether officers followed their department's policy or acted lawfully."[25] Other websites say government-compiled data remain thin and hard to find.[26] Police-involved incidents can spark local protests and national social movements, such as Black Lives Matter. According to Pew, public support

---

[22] Ibid., pages 2–3.
[23] Ibid., page 3.
[24] Ibid., page 6.
[25] https://www.fbi.gov/how-we-can-help-you/more-fbi-services-and-information/ucr/use-of-force
[26] See for example https://mappingpoliceviolence.org/.

for police often correlates with partisanship as well as racial demographics.[27]

There seems to be broad consensus in support of the Supreme Court's decision in *Barnes v. Felix*. The NAACP Legal Defense Fund, the nation's oldest civil rights law organization, filed an amicus brief and later lauded the Supreme Court's unanimous ruling: "today's decision dismantles a dangerous legal framework and is an important step towards advancing police accountability."[28] An essay posted on the Federalist Society websitealso lauded the decision, saying, "a tangled web of judicially confected doctrines often shields egregious governmental misconduct from public scrutiny. A recent Supreme Court decision has brought a significant and welcome shift in this landscape...the Justices unanimously delivered a decisive blow to one of these doctrines—offering a glimmer of hope for greater accountability for law enforcement."[29]

Yet *Barnes v. Felix* did not upend long-standing practices of qualified immunity, a judicial doctrine that protects public officials, including law enforcement officers, from personal liability in civil suits unless they clearly violated a statutory or constitutional right. Qualified immunity remains a complex and controversial ongoing area of public policy debate within states and the US Congress.[30]

An article in *Force Science* explored how the case also avoided thorny police training and reform debates about how officers' actions can contribute to escalating tensions during an encounter. "In practice, this is the

---

[27] Juliana Menasce Horowitz et al., "Views of Race, Policing and Black Lives Matter in the 5 Years Since George Floyd's Killing, *Pew Research Center*, May 7, 2025, https://www.pewresearch.org/race-and-ethnicity/2025/05/07/views-of-race-policing-and-black-lives-matter-in-the-5-years-since-george-floyds-killing/.

[28] "LDF Applauds Supreme Court Decision Advancing Police Accountability," May 16, 2025, https://www.naacpldf.org/press-release/ldf-applauds-supreme-court-decision-advancing-police-accountability/.

[29] Michael Z. Fox, "Keeping Cops Accountable: Supreme Court Issues Decision in Barnes v. Felix," *Federalist Society Blog*, May 21, 2025, https://fedsoc.org/commentary/fedsoc-blog/keeping-cops-accountable-supreme-court-issues-decision-in-barnes-v-felix.

[30] Lawrence Hurley, "Five years after George Floyd's death, calls to reform qualified immunity mostly fall silent," *NBC News*, May 20, 2025, https://www.nbcnews.com/politics/supreme-court/five-years-george-floyds-death-calls-reform-qualified-immunity-mostly-rcna205338.

core of the officer-created jeopardy argument: that if an officer's earlier tactics can be said to have created or increased the risk of danger, then the officer loses the right of self-defense. But that's not what the Supreme Court said in *Barnes v. Felix*. In fact, they went out of their way *not* to say it."[31]

---

[31] Von Kliem, "Barnes v. Felix Exposes the False Dichotomy of 'Moment of Decision' vs. Totality of the Circumstances," *Force Science*, May 22, 2025, emphasis in the original, https://www.forcescience.com/2025/05/barnes-v-felix-exposes-the-false-dichotomy-of-moment-of-decision-vs-totality-of-the-circumstances/#:~:text=Resolving%20the%20 Inconsistency,enforcement%20and%20crime%20prevention%20functions.

CHAPTER 10

TikTok v. *Garland*: The Supreme Court's Ongoing Struggle to Embrace the Impact of Technology Continues

Mark Rush

At first glance, *TikTok* v. *Garland* appears to be an unremarkable First Amendment case that draws upon traditions of tiered judicial scrutiny and fundamental rights analysis. Yet, I suggest that the implications of the case are quite far-reaching.

Those implications are driven by changes taking place in constitutionally exogenous phenomena. In this case that phenomenon is technology. I therefore relate *TikTok* to recent decisions in *NetChoice* v. *Paxton* (2024),[1] *United States* v. *Stevens* (2010),[2] *Brown* v. *Entertainment Merchants*

[1] 603 U.S. 707.
[2] 559 U.S. 460.

M. Rush (✉)
Washington and Lee University, Lexington, VA, USA
e-mail: Rushm@wlu.edu

© The Author(s), under exclusive license to Springer Nature Switzerland AG 2026
H. Schweber (ed.), *SCOTUS 2025*,
https://doi.org/10.1007/978-3-032-10231-7_10

Association (2011),³ and *Kyllo* v. *United States* (2001).⁴ As well, I note and compare the conversations in these cases to the similar conversation between Justice Brandeis and Taft in *Olmstead* v. *United States* (1928).⁵ *Olmstead* addressed the impact of technology—back then, the impact of the telephone—on the balance between governmental surveillance powers and individual privacy rights. In each of the other, twenty-first-century precedents, the Court debated—but did not reach an accord with regard to—whether and how to expand the scope and definition of the powers and rights at stake.

In *TikTok*, there is much less debate and disagreement. At a time when divisions in the Court are quite newsworthy, *TikTok* was an uncharacteristically harmonious decision. It was issued *per curiam* with two brief concurrences by Justices Sotomayor and Gorsuch that addressed definitional matters. Yet, those definitional matters and the Court's careful, painstaking emphasis that the decision was narrow and limited left much unsaid and hanging with regard to the impact to technology on constitutional development and canons of interpretation. Accordingly, *TikTok* is another case in a series of decisions dealing with technology that will lead to a radical sea change in the Court's management of the balance between governmental powers and individual rights.

Background and Decision

In 2021, President Trump issued an Executive Order in which he declared that "the spread in the United States of mobile applications developed and owned by companies in [China] continues to threaten the national security, foreign policy, and economy of the United States."⁶ The President then ordered ByteDance Ltd. to divest all interests in TikTok. Subsequently, Congress enacted the Protecting Americans from Foreign Adversary Controlled Applications Act⁷ which made it "unlawful for any entity to provide certain services to distribute, maintain, or update a foreign adversary controlled application in the United States."⁸

---

³ 564 U.S. 786.
⁴ 533 U.S. 27.
⁵ 277 U.S. 438.
⁶ Slip op. 3, citing Executive Order No.. 13942, 3 CFR 412 (2021).
⁷ Pub. L. 118-50, div. H, 138 Stat. 955.
⁸ Slip. Op. 4.

TikTok claimed that these were squarely speech restrictions cloaked in the garb of business regulation. The government contended that they were business regulations driven by national security concerns that could—but not necessarily did—have downstream impacts on free speech. The Supreme Court gave the government the benefit of the doubt and asserted the narrowness of its decision by noting that while it had not yet "articulated a clear framework for determining whether a regulation of non-expressive activity that disproportionately burdens those engaged in expressive activity triggers heightened review," it would not do so in this case.[9]

The Court rejected TikTok's claim that this was a speech regulation in disguise: "requiring divestiture for the purpose of preventing a foreign adversary from accessing the sensitive data of 170 million U. S. TikTok users is not a subtle means of exercising a content preference."[10] Accordingly, the Court concluded that, as applied to petitioners, "the Act satisfies intermediate scrutiny. The challenged provisions further an important Government interest [countering China's data collection and content manipulation efforts] unrelated to the suppression of free expression and do not burden substantially more speech than necessary to further that interest."[11]

In her concurrence, Justice Sotomayor said that the Court should have looked at the case through the lens of strict scrutiny since it entailed the imposition of a "disproportionate burden" on TikTok. To the extent that TikTok is a social media platform that "engages in expressive activity by compiling and curating material,"[12] and "the Act implicates content creators' right to associate with their preferred publisher for the purpose of speaking,"[13] she suggested that the Court should have applied stricter scrutiny to the challenged regulations.

Gorsuch's concurrence was more extensive. Echoing Sotomayor's concerns, he noted that "even as times and technologies change, the principle of the right to free speech is always the same."[14] He therefore harbored "serious reservations about whether the law before us is content neutral."[15]

[9] Slip Op. 9.
[10] Slip Op 12, internal citations omitted.
[11] Slip. Op. 13.
[12] Slip Op., 1.
[13] Ibid., 2.
[14] Slip. Op. 2.
[15] Ibid.

Yet, he was persuaded the law did further "a compelling interest" and was "appropriately tailored to the problem it seeks to address."[16] But, both concurred in the result. Accordingly, the divisions among the justices were minor and focused principally on definitions.

Context: Simplicity

On the one hand, this decision is almost unremarkable. It fits neatly into two jurisprudential traditions. With regard to the impact the challenged law had on speech, the government had a compelling national security interest. It chose a narrow legislative means of pursuing it that entailed regulating nonspeech activity. The incidental impact on free expression was attenuated at best. So, in this regard, requiring divestiture from TikTok compared to forbidding the burning of draft cards once upon a time in *United States* v. *O'Brien*.[17] In that case, the government had a compelling interest in preserving draft cards. Criminalizing their defacement had an attenuated impact on one of many manners of expressing opposition to the draft and the war in Vietnam.

Second, insofar as this was essentially a case concerning foreign affairs and national security, the Court's deference to the elected branches was also an acknowledgment that they were operating at their highest level of constitutional justification. As Justice Jackson noted in his concurrence in *Youngstown* v. *Sawyer*,[18] when the president acts with the explicit or implied authorization of Congress, his power is at its highest. This was the case in TikTok as both the president and Congress agreed about the threat TikTok posed to national security. Congress supported the president's executive order and followed it with appropriate legislation.

Context: What Is Left Hanging

While the Court sought to place the decision within the confines of these familiar jurisprudential traditions, it also noted that those familiar confines took place in the midst of vast, unprecedented, and uncharted territory. The Court acknowledged this at the outset of the opinion. Citing 80-year-old observations by Justice Frankfurter, the Court compared the novel

---

[16] Ibid., 3–4.
[17] 391 U.S. 367 (1968).
[18] 343 U.S. 579, 635–37 (1952), Jackson concurring.

issues posed by social media platforms to those that arose in the wake of air travel in the mid-twentieth century.

> [W]e are conscious that the cases before us involve new technologies with transformative capabilities. This challenging new context counsels caution on our part. As Justice Frankfurter advised 80 years ago in considering the application of established legal rules to the "totally new problems" raised by the airplane and radio, we should take care not to "embarrass the future." That caution is heightened in these cases, given the expedited time allowed for our consideration. Our analysis must be understood to be narrowly focused in light of these circumstances.[19]

Frankfurter alluded to "embarrassing the future" in *Northwest Airlines, Inc. v. Minnesota*.[20] There, the Court struggled with the disruptive impact that technology—in the form of interstate air travel—had on the firmly established tenets of taxation. The existing rules, he said, were specifically developed to deal with "land commerce."

> To what extent [they] should be carried over to the totally new problems presented by the very different modes of transportation and communication that the airplane and the radio have already introduced, let alone the still more subtle and complicated technological facilities that are on the horizon, raises questions that we ought not to anticipate; certainly we ought not to embarrass the future by judicial answers which, at best, can deal only in a truncated way with problems sufficiently difficult even for legislative statesmanship.[21]

Thanks to the impact of air travel, the Court had to revisit its analysis of the powers of states to tax interstate commerce. Advancements in a constitutionally exogenous variable—technology—disrupted the traditions of interpretation. Yet, the Court divided 5–4 and debated the extent to which Minnesota's taxation for Northwest Airlines was, in fact, a disguised attempt by a state to discriminate against interstate commerce. In this regard, TikTok's assertion that the legislation was a speech restriction in disguise echoed the contentions of Northwest Airlines that the government could not be trusted.

---

[19] Slip Op. 1–2. Internal citations omitted.
[20] 322 U.S. 292 (1944).
[21] Ibid., 300.

So, in addressing whether the executive order and legislation in *TikTok* were, in fact, restrictions on speech, the Court acknowledged that under unprecedented circumstances, it was necessary to reconsider previous jurisprudence and analysis. Insofar as technological advances and the advent of social media had enabled platforms to collect, track, and disseminate personal data, and insofar as another country (in this case, a foreign adversary, China) could use that capacity, it posed an unprecedented national security threat. In addition, the Court had to address the extent to which the use and advancement of technology had any impact on its jurisprudence concerning the scope and definition of speech and privacy rights as well as concerns about national security.

The Impact of Technology on the Definition of Rights and the Court's Trust in the Elected Branches

Changes in technology can alter the constitutional landscape. Therefore the Court has had to account for their impact on the scope of governmental powers and the scope and definition of the rights those powers affect. Perhaps the first detailed discussion of this took place between Justice Brandeis and Chief Justice Taft in *Olmstead* v. *United States*.[22] There, the Chief Justice essentially equated the use of the telephone with shouting out the window. Accordingly, he did not see any reasonable expectation of privacy and, therefore, declared it was unnecessary for the government to get a warrant to tap the phone lines.

> By the invention of the telephone, fifty years ago, and its application for the purpose of extending communications, one can talk with another at a far distant place. The language of the Amendment cannot be extended and expanded to include telephone wires reaching to the whole world from the defendant's house or office. The intervening wires are not part of his house or office any more than are the highways along which they are stretched.[23]

Brandeis disagreed and argued that the protections of the right to privacy had to be recalibrated to be commensurate with the augmented scope of government surveillance power.

---

[22] 277 U.S. 438 (1928).
[23] Ibid., 465.

> [T]ime works changes, brings into existence new conditions and purposes. Subtler and more far-reaching means of invading privacy have become available to the Government. Discovery and invention have made it possible for the Government, by means far more effective than stretching upon the rack, to obtain disclosure in court of what is whispered in the closet.[24]

Ultimately, Brandeis was vindicated in *Katz* v. *United States*,[25] where the Court declared that wiretaps required a warrant.

A similar discussion took place in *Kyllo* v. *United States*.[26] There, the Court had to decide whether the use of thermal imaging devices constituted a "search" for the purposes of the Fourth Amendment. The Court declared that this was the case. Therefore, the use of thermal imaging devices did require a warrant. Writing for the Court, Justice Scalia echoed Brandeis and stated, "It would be foolish to contend that the degree of privacy secured to citizens by the Fourth Amendment has been entirely unaffected by the advance of technology."[27]

Yet, in *Brown* v. *Entertainment Merchants Association*,[28] Scalia said exactly the opposite with regard to the harm caused by speech in violent video games: "whatever the challenges of applying the Constitution to ever-advancing technology, the basic principles of freedom of speech and the press, like the First Amendment's command, do not vary when a new and different medium for communication appears."[29]

Thus, in seeking not to "embarrass the future," the *TikTok* Court took pains to acknowledge that it was not going to address whether the social media platform's engagement in speech-related activity shielded it from accountability for the harm that could be caused by a foreign government's access to its data collection recourses. Since this was new territory, the Court deferred to the judgment of Congress and the Executive:

> Rather than meaningfully dispute the scope of the data TikTok collects or the ends to which it may be used, petitioners contest probability, asserting that it is "unlikely" that China would compel TikTok to turn over user data

---

[24] Ibid., 473–474.
[25] 389 U.S. 347 (1967).
[26] 533 U.S. 27 (2001).
[27] Ibid., 34.
[28] 564 U.S. 786 (2011).
[29] 790 internal citations omitted. In *Brown*, then, Scalia foreshadowed and echoed Gorsuch's concerns in his *TikTok* concurrence. In *Kyllo*, he contradicted Gorsuch.

for intelligence-gathering purposes, since China has more effective and efficient means of obtaining relevant information. In reviewing the constitutionality of the Act, however, we must accord substantial deference to the predictive judgments of Congress. Sound policymaking often requires legislators to forecast future events and to anticipate the likely impact of these events based on deductions and inferences for which complete empirical support may be unavailable.[30]

This, again, is in stark contrast to the Court's dismissal of such "predictive" judgments made by the California legislature when assessing the causal link between children's violent behavior and the violence they witness and engage in video games. Writing for the Court in *Brown*, Scalia rejected the possibility that "the legislature can make a *predictive judgment* that such a link exists."[31]

Is This a National Security Emergency or Paradigm Shift?

This apparent inconsistency regarding predictive legislative judgments might be resolvable based on the extent to which *TikTok* involved foreign affairs and a threat to national security, whereas *Kyllo* and *Brown* did not. As well, none of the cases posed an emergent threat. In *TikTok*, the plausible, palpable threat to national security tipped the balance in favor of Congress.

> Here, the Government's TikTok-related data collection concerns do not exist in isolation. The record reflects that China "has engaged in extensive and years-long efforts to accumulate structured datasets, in particular on U. S. persons, to support its intelligence and counterintelligence operations."
>
> Even if China has not yet leveraged its relationship with ByteDance Ltd. to access U. S. TikTok users' data, petitioners offer no basis for concluding that the Government's determination that China might do so is not at least a reasonable inference based on substantial evidence. We are mindful that this law arises in a context in which national security and foreign policy concerns arise in connection with efforts to confront evolving threats in an area where information can be difficult to obtain and the impact of certain conduct dif-

---

[30] *TikTok*, slip op. 14.
[31] *Brown*, 799 emphasis added.

ficult to assess. We thus afford the Government's "informed judgment" substantial respect here.[32]

Conclusion: Going Not So Boldly Where the Court Has Not Gone Before

TikTok and the other cases I mention share a common concern about the enhanced threats posed to individual rights posed by the technologically enhanced power of the government and private entities such as social media platforms. The novelty of these challenges has produced inconsistent judicial reasoning.

1. The existence of a *bona fide* national security/foreign affairs threat resulted in the Court's deferring to the government's restrictions on platforms based on "predictive" analysis (*TikTok*).
2. Absent that national security threat, the Court has been less solicitous of legislative restrictions on technologically enhanced speech-based harms.
3. The Court has expressed a clear understanding that technology has enhanced threats to privacy and either restricted government surveillance power (*Kyllo*) or allowed the government to restrict the privacy threats posed by social media platforms (*TikTok*).
4. But, absent a national security/foreign affairs threat, governments may not prevent the social media platforms from restricting their users' speech (*NetChoice* v. *Paxton*) because the platforms are engaged in their own speech when doing so.[33]

These contradictions raise important questions that the Court will inevitably address. As technology continues to develop, it will produce more challenges to speech and privacy. This will raise additional questions about whether the contextual distinction between domestic and foreign affairs should matter to the Court when the threat or harm posed by technology is either emergent or could become so.

---

[32] *TikTok* 14–15. Internal citations omitted.
[33] 603 U.S. 707 (2024). See also Rush, Mark, "NetChoice v. Paxton: Navigating and Refereeing Freedom of Speech in Cyberspace" in Schweber, Howard, ed., *SCOTUS 2024*. Springer. Available: https://www.springerprofessional.de/en/scotus-2024/50730136#TOC.

Accordingly, I suggest that the Court's jurisprudence concerning technology, surveillance, social media platforms, and speech is at a critical juncture. The objects of the threats posed by technologically enhanced speech or surveillance are threatened with the same harms regardless of their source. Thus, as the Court moves forward, it will become necessary for the justices to focus on what unites such cases—technologically based threats—instead of the national or international context which divides them. Technology transcends the national borders that once enabled the Court to distinguish its conclusions about government powers and individual rights.

CHAPTER 11

Oklahoma Statewide Charter School Board v. Drummond: Religious Charter Schools at an Impasse

Lauren Gilbert

In a highly anticipated opinion,[1] on May 22, 2025, the US Supreme Court (SCOTUS) in a brief 4–4 decision left for another day the question of whether States may or must allow religious charter schools. Notwithstanding a trilogy of cases finding that under the Free Exercise Clause (FEC), states cannot deny a public benefit to religious schools that they grant to other

---

[1] Mark Walsh, *Supreme Court Case Could Reshape Landscape for Charter and Religious Schools*, Education Week (April 28, 2025). Approximately sixty amicus briefs were filed with SCOTUS. Oklahoma Statewide Charter School Board v. Drummond, No. 24-394, https://www.supremecourt.gov/search.aspx?filename=/docket/docketfiles/html/public/24-396.html.

L. Gilbert (✉)
Independent Scholar previously Professor of Law, St. Thomas University College of Law, USA, Miami Gardens, FL

© The Author(s), under exclusive license to Springer Nature Switzerland AG 2026
H. Schweber (ed.), *SCOTUS 2025*,
https://doi.org/10.1007/978-3-032-10231-7_11

private schools,[2] SCOTUS deadlocked over whether to extend that rule to public charter schools after Justice Amy Coney Barrett recused herself and a conservative justice joined the liberal justices in voting to affirm the Oklahoma Supreme Court's ruling invalidating the charter of a religious school.[3] Justice Barrett, previously a Notre Dame law professor, may have recused herself because Notre Dame's Religious Liberties Clinic represented St. Isidore of Seville (St. Isidore's), the proposed religious charter school, or, more probably, because Professor Nicole Stelle Garnette, a Notre Dame colleague, fellow law clerk, and friend, was advising attorneys representing the school.[4] As a result, whether denying public charters to religious schools violates the FEC remains an unresolved issue to be decided by lower courts with rulings that apply only within their respective jurisdictions.

---

[2] *See* Trinity Lutheran Church of Columbia, Inc. v. Comer, 582 U.S. 449 (2017) (state program offering grants to schools for playground resurfacing but denying funding to Trinity Lutheran school because of its religious character violated the FEC); Espinoza v. Montana Dep't of Revenue, 591 U.S. 464 (2020) ("a state need not subsidize private education ... [b]ut once a state decides to do so, it cannot disqualify some private schools solely because they are religious"); Carson as next friend of O. C. v. Makin, 596 U.S. 767 (2022) (Maine's tuition assistance program was subject to free exercise principles governing any public benefit program including prohibiting the denial of a benefit because of a recipient's religious exercise).

[3] Oklahoma Statewide Charter School Board v. Drummond, 145 S.Ct. 1916 (2025). The affirmance did not indicate how the justices voted.

[4] *See, e.g.*, Linda Jacobson, *The Justice, the Professor and the Friendship That Could Rattle a Pivotal Religious Charter School Case*, The 74 (March 17, 2025). Although Chief Justice Roberts, who had authored each case in the trilogy, may have cast the tie vote, the conservative media, including the *Wall Street Journal* and *The National Review*, blamed Justice Barrett for the outcome. *See* Dan McLaughlin, *Justice Barrett's Recusal Leads to Defeat for Oklahoma Religious Charter School*, The National Review (May 22, 2025); Editorial Board, *A Religious Charter School Falls Short at the Supreme Court*, Wall St. J. (May 22, 2025).

ORIGINS OF CHARTER SCHOOLS AND THE SCHOOL CHOICE MOVEMENT

Parents' right to control the education of their children has long been recognized as a protected liberty interest under the Constitution.[5] Over 100 years ago, SCOTUS struck down a state law mandating public school attendance between the ages of 8 and 16 years.[6] The Court wrote:

> The fundamental theory of liberty upon which all governments in this Union repose excludes any general power of the state to standardize its children by forcing them to accept instruction from public teachers only.[7]

Over the last 30 years, *school choice* has become a nationwide movement defined by letting parents decide the best means of educating their children in elementary and secondary school, whether it be in a traditional public school, charter school, private school, or homeschooling. Recently, it has come to include supporting that choice through government funding, including of religiously affiliated schools.

The city of St. Paul, Minnesota, created the first charter school in 1992 after the state legislature passed a charter schools law in 1991.[8] Over the last quarter-century, the number of charter schools has grown, with a reported 7800 charter schools today in 47 states.[9] Thus far, virtually all states with charter school laws require that education at charter schools be nonsectarian. In contrast, a smaller but growing number of states have voucher programs,[10] --essentially scholarships which can be used at religious or secular private schools.[11]

School choice has become the rallying cry not only for charter schools and voucher programs but also for home-schooling and even opt-outs

---

[5] *See* Meyer v. Nebraska, 262 U.S. 390 (1923) (struck down English-only law in public and private schools).
[6] Pierce v. Society of the Sisters of the Holy Names of Jesus and Mary, 268 U.S. 510 (1925).
[7] *Id.* at 535.
[8] Laws of Minnesota 1991, ch. 265, art. 9, sect. 3.
[9] *See* Rebecca R. Skinner & Isobel Sorenson, *Overview of Public and Private School Choice Options*, Cong. Rsch. Serv. 1 (updated May 23, 2025) (hereinafter "*Overview of School Choice Options*").
[10] *Id.* at 2.
[11] *Cf. Carson*, 596 U.S. at 774–775.

from certain subjects in public school[12] as many parents reject traditional public schools because of the quality of the education or fundamental disagreement with the values being taught. In February 2017, in his first joint address to Congress, President Donald J. Trump called for

> an education bill that funds school choice *for disadvantaged youth, including millions of African American and Latino children.* These families should be free to choose the public, private, charter, magnet, religious, or home school that is right for them.[13]

Eight years later, in 2025, when Congress approved the first national school voucher plan, it offered school vouchers to all but the wealthiest parents.[14] Focused in its early stages on poorer children in failing schools, *school choice* now aims to make public funding available to nearly all students seeking alternatives to traditional public schools. Religiously affiliated charter schools are the next, if not final, frontier.

The Relevant Cases

After *Brown v. Board of Education*,[15] with segregated public schools under court orders to pursue integration "with all deliberate speed,"[16] many white parents moved their children into white-only private schools, which often were religiously affiliated.[17] State funding of white-only schools was challenged under the Fourteenth Amendment's equal protection clause[18]

---

[12] Mahmoud v. Taylor, 145 S.Ct. 2332 (2025) (granting preliminary injunction to parents seeking opt-outs from LGBTQ+ inclusive storybooks).

[13] *Remarks by President Trump in Joint Address to Congress*, 1 Pub. Papers 1 (Feb. 28, 2017) (emphasis added).

[14] Sarah Mervosh and Dana Goldstein, *Congress Passes a National School Voucher Program*, N.Y. Times (July 3, 2025).

[15] 347 U.S. 483 (1954) ("Brown I").

[16] Brown v. Board of Education, 349 U.S. 294, 301 (1955) ("Brown II").

[17] Diane Ravitch, *The Dark History of School Choice*, New York Rev. Books (Jan. 14, 2021) (book review).

[18] In *Norwood v. Harris*, 413 U.S. 455 (1973), SCOTUS struck down Mississippi's textbook-lending program to schools, including white-only private schools, on the basis that a "State's constitutional obligation requires it to steer clear, not only of operating the old dual system of racially segregated schools, but also of giving significant aid to institutions that practice racial or other invidious discrimination." *Id.* at 467. *But see* Allen v. Wright, 468 U.S. 737 (1984) (parents' challenge to IRS regulations as not adopting sufficient standards to deny tax-exempt status to racially discriminatory schools dismissed for lack of standing).

while public funding of religious schools was challenged under the Establishment Clause. Against that backdrop, in 1971, SCOTUS created the *Lemon* Test, using it to strike down two states' statutes providing state aid to religious primary and secondary schools in the form of subsidies for teachers' salaries.[19] SCOTUS ruled that public support for religion violated the Establishment Clause unless the Government could show that (1) the law had a secular (non-religious) purpose; (2) the law had neither the purpose nor effect of aiding or inhibiting religion; *and* (3) there was no excessive government entanglement with religion.[20] Gradually, the Court moved away from the three-part *Lemon* Test, often focusing on whether state action was a *symbolic endorsement* of religion.[21] The Court explicitly rejected both tests in 2022 when it decided *Kennedy v. Bremerton School District*,[22] asserting that "this Court long ago abandoned *Lemon* and its endorsement test offshoot."[23] Instead, Justice Gorsuch wrote, "this Court has instructed that the Establishment Clause must be interpreted by 'reference to historical practices and understandings'."[24]

Oklahoma's Charter School Program

Oklahoma's Constitution has a no aid provision. It states in relevant part that

> No public money ... shall ever be appropriated, applied, donated, or used, directly or indirectly, for the use ... of any sect, church, denomination, or system of religion, or for the use, benefit, or support of any ... religious teacher ... or sectarian institution as such.[25]

---

[19] Lemon v. Kurtzman, 403 U.S. 602 (1971).

[20] *Id.* at 612–613.

[21] *See, e.g.,* Lynch v. Donnelly, 465 U.S. 668, 694 (1984); County of Allegheny v. Greater Pittsburgh ACLU, 492 U.S. 573, 627 (1989) (O'Connor, J., concurring in part and concurring in the judgment).

[22] 597 U.S. 507 (2022) (School violated Coach Kennedy's First Amendment rights when it sought to proscribe him from "engaging in a brief, quiet, personal religious observance doubly protected by the Free Exercise and Free Speech Clauses" on the basis that allowing him to pray in the middle of the field at the game's end would symbolically endorse religion).

[23] *Id.* at 534.

[24] *Id.* at 535 (citing to Town of Greece v. Galloway, 572 U.S. 565, 576 (2014)).

[25] Oka. Const., art. 2, §5.

Oklahoma's Constitution also provides that "[p]rovision shall be made for the establishment and maintenance of a system of *free public schools*, which shall be open to all the children of the State *and free from sectarian control.*"[26] In 1999, the Legislature enacted the Oklahoma Charter Schools Act (the Act).[27] The goals of the Act included providing for academic choice for parents and children.[28] The Act provides that a charter school, which it defined as a *"public school* established by contract" with a qualifying entity, should be nonsectarian in its programs, admissions policies, employment practices, and all other operations.[29]

The Archdiocese of Oklahoma City and the Diocese of the City of Tulsa applied to the Statewide Virtual Charter School Board (SVCSB) to establish St. Isidore's as a virtual (or online) charter school. The stated purpose was "'[t]o create, establish and operate' the school as a Catholic School."[30]

On June 5, 2023, the SVCSB voted 3–2 to approve St. Isidore's application to become a virtual charter school, free to exercise its religious beliefs and practices consistent with religious protections. On October 9, 2023, SVCSB voted 3–2 to approve St. Isidore's proposed contract, which the parties executed on October 16, 2023.[31]

The Oklahoma Attorney General, acting on the State's behalf, petitioned the Oklahoma Supreme Court (OKSCt) for a writ of mandamus directing SVCSB to rescind the contract. OKSCt accepted the case based on its original jurisdiction as a matter of public interest warranting immediate action.

THE OKLAHOMA SUPREME COURT DECISION

OKSCt found that the contract was invalid under Oklahoma's Constitution, Oklahoma's Charter Schools Act, and the Establishment Clause.[32] Its Constitution required the legislature to establish and maintain a system of

---

[26] Okla. Const., art. 1, § 5 (emphasis added).
[27] 70 O.S. Supp. 2023, §§ 70-3-130 et seq.
[28] *Id.* at § 70-3-131.
[29] *Id.* at §§ 70-3-132.2(C)(1)(emphasis added), 136A)(2).
[30] Drummond ex rel. State v. Oklahoma Statewide Virtual Charter School Board, 558 P.3d 1, 6 (2024).
[31] *Id.* at 6–7.
[32] *Id.* at 15.

free public schools, mandating that they be nonsectarian.[33] It also prohibited the State from appropriating or using any public money for the "use, benefit or support" of any sectarian institution.[34] The Act prohibited the Charter School Board from "sponsoring a charter school program that is affiliated with a nonpublic sectarian school or religious institution."[35] OKSCt found that "[t]here is no question that St. Isidore is a sectarian institution and will be sectarian in its programs and operations."[36]

Six of the nine OKSCt justices concurred, but one justice wrote a lengthy dissent. She argued that allowing religious organizations to contract with the State to provide educational services did not violate the no aid provision of Oklahoma's Constitution or the First Amendment's Establishment Clause.[37] Insofar as the Act denied religious organizations the opportunity to apply to operate charter schools, it violated the FEC.[38]

SCOTUS DIVIDED ON RELIGIOUS CHARTER SCHOOLS

SCOTUS deadlocked 4–4 in reviewing the OKSCt's ruling. Although the American Civil Liberties Union hailed the decision as a victory for public schools and the separation of church and state,[39] this was hyperbole. In fact, SCOTUS kicked the ball down the road. So why did five justices not vote in favor of chartering St. Isidore's? Prior to SCOTUS's decision, one author pointed out that

> the Court has consistently expanded the scope of the Free Exercise Clause at the expense of the Establishment Clause. If the Supreme Court orders the State of Oklahoma to create a religious public school by contract, it is effectively rendering the rights conferred in the Establishment Clause null and void.[40]

---

[33] *Id.* at 9.
[34] *Id.* at 7.
[35] *Id.* at 9.
[36] *Id.*
[37] *Id.* at 15 (J. Huehn, dissenting).
[38] *Id.* at 18.
[39] Press Release, *Supreme Court Affirms Oklahoma Supreme Court Ruling Rejecting Nation's First Religious Public Charter School*, American Civil Liberties Union (May 22, 2025).
[40] Alisha Camacho Clegg, *A Clash of the Clauses: The Constitutionality of the Nation's First Religious Public Charter School*, 77 Okla. L. Rev. 627, 668 (Spring 2025).

It may be that Chief Justice Roberts, who had carefully constructed the Free Exercise trilogy, wanted a more incremental case to extend the nondiscrimination rule in *Carson v. Makin* to religious charter schools. Perhaps SCOTUS overturning the OKSCt and mandating the creation of St. Isidore's was a bridge too far, considering St. Isidore's plans to fully integrate Catholic social teaching throughout the curriculum.[41] Or perhaps, Roberts was just waiting for Justice Barrett and a solid 6–3 majority.

As a majority of the OKSCt no doubt recognized, the trilogy of cases elevating the FEC over the Establishment Clause was a departure from precedent and at odds with many states' long-standing no aid provisions barring government funding of sectarian schools. In November 2016, when Oklahoma voters had the opportunity to amend their Constitution to repeal the no aid provision, they rejected it.[42] A year later, in *Trinity Lutheran*, Chief Justice Roberts set out to accomplish via the power of judicial review what had not been achieved through the political process, culminating in the effective nullification of state no aid provisions via *Carson v. Makin*. The contract for a religious public charter school proved in the end, however, to be a step SCOTUS was not yet prepared to take.

During oral argument, Justice Alito asked whether the State was showing hostility toward religion in refusing to charter St. Isidore's. He referenced the statement by Oklahoma's Attorney General that if they allowed Christian schools they would have to allow other religious charter schools which Christians would not want to support with their tax dollars.[43] The attorney for Oklahoma replied that this was not the Attorney General's perspective, but rather he was explaining why we need an Establishment Clause: to avoid the religious strife that occurs when the government appears to favor one religion over another.[44] This same point was raised by Justice Kagan, who argued that once you allow free religious charter schools, other religions will apply, and claims of discrimination will follow when certain religions appear to be favored over others.[45]

---

[41] St. Isidore of Seville Catholic Virtual School v. Drummond, No. 24-396, petition for cert. (App. 201a-206a) (Oct. 7, 2024) (excerpts from application).

[42] *State Question 790: Voters say public money can't be used for religious purposes*, Tulsa World (Nov. 8, 2016).

[43] Oklahoma Statewide Charter School Board v. Drummond, No. 24-394 and No. 24-396, Oral Argument at 125–126 (U.S. April 30, 2024).

[44] *Id.* at 126–127.

[45] *Id.* at 79–80.

Justice Gorsuch, who wrote the opinion that scrapped the *Lemon* Test, finding that the proper test was "reference to historical practices and understandings,"[46] noted that prior to adoption of state Blaine Amendments,[47] many states had their own FECs but also a history of denying funding to religious schools.[48] Lawyers for the school argued that the history was not particularly useful because it was motivated by anti-Catholic bias, and because prior to the adoption of the Fourteenth Amendment in 1868 the Constitution's religion clauses were not enforceable against the States.[49]

It is noteworthy that Oklahoma did not become a state until 1907 and the no aid provision in its Constitution was imposed upon it as a condition of statehood.[50] Yet ironically, more than a century later, in 2016, when Oklahoma voters had the opportunity to pass a constitutional amendment repealing the no aid provision, they rejected it.[51] Not long thereafter, Justice Roberts began to craft the reasoning that would allow SCOTUS to reinterpret the FEC to invalidate no aid provisions in state constitutions and laws across the country. Once again, SCOTUS's power to say what the law is won out over the will of the majority.

Many school choice advocates see religious charter schools as the next, if not final, frontier. They will no doubt take the 4–4 vote as a temporary setback while seeking a stronger vehicle to bring this issue back before SCOTUS. How states structure their charter schools (as public or private) may determine whether they survive the Establishment Clause challenges that are sure to come.

---

[46] *Kennedy v. Bremerton School District*, 597 U.S. at 535.

[47] Most state Blaine Amendments were adopted after the US Senate in 1876 narrowly rejected former House Speaker James G. Blaine's proposed amendment to the Constitution that would have prohibited direct government aid to religious educational institutions. *See* McCarley E. Maddock, *Blaine in the Joints: The History of Blaine Amendments and Modern Supreme Court Religious Liberty Doctrine in Education*, 18 Duke J. Const. L. & Pub. Pol'y 196, 200 (2023).

[48] Oral Argument at 28.

[49] *Id.*

[50] Enabling Act of 1906, Ch. 3335, 59th Cong. § 4 (1st Sess. 1906), *discussed in* Brief of the Rutherford Institute as Amicus Curiae in Support of Petitioners, pp. 12–13, *Okla. Statewide Charter School Board v. Drummond*, Nos. 24-394 and 24-396 (March 12, 2025).

[51] *Oklahoma State Question 790, Repeal of Ban on Public Funding for Religious Institutions Amendment* (2016), Ballotpedia, *available at* https://ballotpedia.org/Oklahoma_State_Question_790,_Repeal_of_Ban_on_Public_Funding_for_Religious_Institutions_Amendment_(2016).

CHAPTER 12

Mahmoud v. Taylor: A New Standard for Religious Accommodation in Public Schools

Carol Nackenoff

INTRODUCTION

What kinds of accommodations do states have to provide for persons or entities seeking religious exemptions from laws or regulations that burden their sincerely held religious beliefs and practices? The First Amendment's command that *"Congress shall make no law respecting an establishment of religion, or prohibiting the free exercise thereof..."* has applied to the states for nearly a century. In *Mahmoud v. Taylor*, the Court answered that question with regard to public schools in a way that is both more protective of free exercise than most prior decisions and that may ultimately be read quite expansively.

In a key free exercise decision from 1990, Justice Scalia's majority opinion explained that when states passed laws that were within the power of government to enact and that are of general applicability, they were not constitutionally required to accommodate religious practices. The

C. Nackenoff (✉)
Swarthmore College, Swarthmore, PA, USA
e-mail: Cnacken1@swarthmore.edu

© The Author(s), under exclusive license to Springer Nature Switzerland AG 2026
H. Schweber (ed.), *SCOTUS 2025*,
https://doi.org/10.1007/978-3-032-10231-7_12

majority held that the most rigorous form of review—requiring a state to demonstrate a compelling interest in a regulation and that it had chosen the least restrictive means of furthering that compelling interest—would be too stringent in the case before them. Scalia wrote in *Employment Division, Department of Human Resources of Oregon v. Smith* that "[a]ny society adopting such a system would be courting anarchy, but that danger increases in direct proportion to the society's diversity of religious beliefs, and its determination to coerce or suppress none of them."[1] Allowing exceptions to every state law or regulation affecting religion "would open the prospect of constitutionally required exemptions from civic obligations of almost every conceivable kind."[2]

This decision, deferential to the government's need to govern, was highly unpopular. It has been whittled away, though not reversed. In reaction to *Smith*, Congress passed the Religious Freedom Restoration Act of 1993 (RFRA) prohibiting any agency, department, or US or state official from substantially burdening a person's exercise of religion even if the burden results from a rule of general applicability. Congress tried, in this Act, to impose strict scrutiny (the compelling interest standard). That same year, Justice Kennedy, writing for the Court in another case, read the *Smith* decision to mean that a law burdening free exercise that is not neutral or generally applicable must be evaluated using the highest level of scrutiny.[3] After the Supreme Court held that the federal RFRA did not apply to the states,[4] a number of states passed their own RFRAs, and some others interpreted their state constitutions to offer similar protections. The Supreme Court would not generally show an appetite for such a high level of scrutiny for free exercise claims for roughly the next fifteen years.

The Roberts Court has become increasingly protective of the free exercise claims of religious adherents.[5] It has been solicitous of religious

---

[1] 494 U.S. 872, 888 (1990). The majority decision rejected the applicability here of *Sherbert v. Verner*'s strict scrutiny standard for laws that made it impossible for religious adherents to access unemployment benefits without violating key tenets of their faith (374 U.S. 398 (1963)) since Oregon had criminalized the use of peyote.

[2] *Smith* at 888.

[3] *Church of the Lukumi Babalu Aye v. City of Hialeah* 508 U.S. 520 (1993).

[4] *City of Boerne v. Flores* 521 U.S. 507 (1997).

[5] The Roberts Court has found free exercise violations in cases including *Trinity Lutheran Church of Columbia v. Comer* 582 U.S. 449 (2017); *Espinoza v. Montana Department of Revenue* 581 U.S. 464 (2020) (Kevin Pybas in *SCOTUS 2020*); *Kennedy v. Bremerton School District* 597 U.S. 507 (2022) (Howard Schweber in *SCOTUS 2022*), *Carson v. Makin* 596 U.S. 767 (2022) (Steven Lichtman in *SCOTUS 2022*).

objections to complying with generally applicable antidiscrimination laws when it means violating beliefs about the sanctity of marriage between biological men and biological women.[6] Regardless of the expansion of some state antidiscrimination laws to include LGBTQ+ persons,[7] the recognition of the right to same-sex marriage as a fundamental liberty under the Fourteenth Amendment,[8] and the Court's decision that workplace discrimination against LGBTQ+ persons because of their gender identity constituted sex discrimination under Title VII of the 1964 Civil Rights Act,[9] antidiscrimination laws and ordinances are frequently treated as unimportant in the face of First Amendment free exercise claims. This includes situations in which religious adherents object to providing paid services for gay weddings that they offer other couples.[10] The Court's willingness to entertain and validate these claims further encouraged interest groups to advance them.

BACKGROUND OF THE CASE

During the 2022–2023 academic year, the Montgomery County Maryland Board of Education, concerned that the county's highly diverse population was not adequately represented in public school materials, introduced five "LGBTQ+-inclusive" books into the pre-K through grade five curriculum. Parents from several religious traditions objected to the requirement that their children be instructed using these materials. Montgomery County Schools had allowed an opt-out at first, but eliminated it because, they said, principals and teachers "could not accommodate the growing number of opt out requests without causing significant disruptions to the

---

[6] See *Fulton v. City of Philadelphia* 593 U.S. 522 (2021) (Meg Penrose in *SCOTUS 2021*), where the Court was invited, but declined, to overturn the *Smith* decision.

[7] A number of states include gender identity or expression or sexual orientation in their antidiscrimination statutes and prohibit discrimination in employment, shopping and eating at businesses open to the public, housing, and public schools. Maryland's antidiscrimination statute (Md. Code. Ann. Educ. § 7-424(a)) includes harassment and bullying on the basis of gender identity in public schools.

[8] *Obergefell v. Hodges* 576 U.S. 644 (2015).

[9] *Bostock v. Clayton County* 590 U.S. 644 (2020) (Julie Novkov in *SCOTUS 2020*).

[10] *Masterpiece Cakeshop. Ltd v. Colorado Civil Rights Commission* 584 U.S. 617 (2018) (Stephen M. Engel in *SCOTUS 2018*) where Colorado was barred from enforcing the state's antidiscrimination act; *303 Creative LLC v. Elenis* 600 U.S. 570 (2023) reached a similar conclusion on free speech grounds (Stacey L. Sobel in *SCOTUS 2023*).

classroom environment."[11] The voluminous requests, they claimed, made administering the curriculum unmanageable. The School District then refused to provide advance notice when the books were going to be used as part of the literacy curriculum.

In *Mahmoud v. Taylor*, parents who sought a preliminary and a permanent injunction claimed the no-opt-out policy infringed on their free exercise rights. Demanding the right to direct their children's religious upbringing, they asserted that the School Board's policy posed "a very real threat of undermining" the religious practices and beliefs they wished to instill in their children, drawing on the Court's 1972 holding with regard to exempting children of the Old Order Amish from mandatory high school attendance until age 16 in *Wisconsin v. Yoder*. The Amish had successfully argued that education beyond eighth grade exposed their children to worldly influences and maintained that their religious community required separation from contemporary society. The state age requirement threatened the survival of their insular community. While holding Wisconsin's age requirement to strict scrutiny in this case, the *Yoder* decision was based on a showing that few other religious groups or sects were thought likely to be able to make.[12] A central issue in *Mahmoud* would be the relevance of *Yoder* to the Montgomery County School Board's literacy curriculum.

Majority Opinion

In *Mahmoud*, the Supreme Court took a major step in expanding the requirement to accommodate parents who asserted the right to direct the religious upbringing of their children according to the sincerely held tenets of their faith. The opinion of the Court, written by Justice Samuel Alito, was joined by Chief Justice Roberts and Justices Thomas, Gorsuch, Kavanaugh, and Barrett—all the conservative justices. Alito wrote that this free exercise right "follow[s] those children into the public school classroom."[13] On same-sex relationships, gay marriage, and gender identity, the books used in the elementary school curriculum were "unmistakably normative ... clearly designed to present certain values and beliefs as things to be celebrated and certain contrary values and beliefs as things to

---

[11] *Mahmoud v. Taylor*, opinion of the Court, slip opinion at 9 quoting one Board official.
[12] Alito, majority opinion, slip opinion, 29.
[13] *Id.*, 17–19, quoting *Espinoza, supra* note 5 at 486.

be rejected."[14] Both the texts themselves (which the majority saw as approving of certain viewpoints) and guidance provided with the books "encouraged teachers to '[d]isrupt the either/or thinking' of their students." Parents felt their children were being encouraged to disregard parental and religious guidance on such matters.[15] Very young children were in no position to reject the views advanced by the authority figure in their classroom.

The majority agreed that the complaining parents were being forced to make a choice between their faith and accessing a public benefit—public education—for which they paid taxes. The government may not condition the availability of a proffered benefit "upon a recipient's willingness to surrender his religiously impelled status."[16] Telling parents they could send their children to private school was no answer since many could not afford to do so.

Justice Alito's opinion placed heavy emphasis on *Wisconsin v. Yoder* (1972) in concluding that the School Board's policy was not simply an incidental burden placed on religious exercise. "[T]he burden imposed is of the same character as that imposed in *Yoder*," and therefore strict scrutiny applies whether or not the policy is neutral and of general applicability.[17] Thus, the *Smith-Church of the Lukumi Babalu Aye* approach to applying or withholding strict scrutiny—based on an evaluation of the neutrality and general applicability of the policy—was unnecessary. A strict scrutiny standard is almost always fatal in fact, and the majority found that this case was no exception. Although the Board asserted an interest in protecting students from "social stigma and isolation," it could not claim to rescue one group of students [LGBTQ+] from stigmatization by stigmatizing and isolating children from religiously conservative families.[18] The fact that the Montgomery County School Board permits opt-outs in a variety of other circumstances, including the "Family Life and Human Sexuality" unit, undermines the Board's claim that providing opt-outs to religious parents would be unworkable.

---

[14] *Id.*, 22.
[15] *Id.* at 7, 12.
[16] *Id.* at 32, quoting *Trinity Lutheran Church, supra* note 5 at 462.
[17] Alito, slip opinion, 36.
[18] *Id.*, at 39.

The Court held that the parents bringing the case were entitled to the preliminary injunction they seek while the lawsuit against the Board of Education proceeds.

In a separate concurrence, Justice Thomas deemed sex education in public schools a twentieth-century invention, with sexual and gender identity education for young children of even more recent origin. Neither was part of state-sponsored education's historical pedigree. He read a number of cases as rejecting the idea that promoting ideological conformity among citizens is a legitimate state interest.[19]

Dissent

Justice Sonia Sotomayor's dissent, joined by Justices Kagan and Jackson, strongly objected to what they saw as the majority's misreading and extension of *Yoder* to establish a novel "threat" test. Instead, *Yoder* "compelled Amish parents to do what their religion forbade: send their children away [to high school] rather than integrate them into the Amish community at home."[20]

The dissenters predicted chaos for the nation's public schools, claiming the ruling "threatens the very essence of public education."[21] Schooling promotes the nation's common destiny and creates a practice of living in our multicultural society, and the school district introduced the materials to encourage "mutual tolerance and 'respect' for all those in the community." Books like *Uncle Bobby's Wedding* would be used the same way as other books in the English language program, and exposure is not coercion.[22]

The dissenters saw a major break with free exercise precedent: "Exposing students to the 'message' that LGBTQ people exist and that their loved ones may celebrate their marriages and life events, the majority says, is enough to trigger the most demanding form of judicial scrutiny."[23] The Free Exercise Clause bars government from compelling individuals to

---

[19] Thomas concurrence, 7, 10–11 with special reference to *Pierce v. Society of Sisters* 268 U.S. 510 (1925).
[20] Sotomayor, dissent, slip opinion, 14–15.
[21] *Id.* at 2, 38.
[22] *Id.* at 6, 21.
[23] *Id.* at 1.

violate or give up their religious beliefs but does not guarantee that citizens can avoid ideas with which they disagree.[24] For the dissenters, Justice Alito's reading of *Yoder*, and the novel "threat" test the majority invents in *Mahmoud*, "imposes no meaningful limits on the types of school decisions subject to strict scrutiny."[25] As a result of this decision, schools are likely to censor their curricula.

"[R]equiring schools to provide advance notice and the chance to opt out of every lesson plan or story time that might implicate a parent's religious beliefs will impose impossible administrative burdens on schools."[26] In Montgomery County, a multilevel appeals process for parents to challenge objectionable library books and instructional materials was already in place. Dissenters expressed concern that the chief locus of decision-making about public education policy, traditionally lodged with democratically elected officials at the state and local level, is being usurped by a Court that lacks knowledge and experience in education policy. This, Sotomayor argues, is an exercise in judicial maximalism.[27]

Looking Forward

A state's failure to accommodate sincerely held religious beliefs in public schools must now be examined using strict scrutiny. *Yoder*'s compelling state interest standard, which had previously been relied upon quite sparingly by the Court, has now been elevated to center stage when considering threats to free exercise in public education.

The dissent's concern that the test in *Mahmoud* "lacks any meaningful limit"[28] and reaches far more than LGBTQ+ acceptance does not seem far-fetched. Justice Sotomayor's parade of horribles (in some cases, drawing on issues that have come before lower courts) included parental religious objections to curricular mentions of women working outside the home or of women's accomplishments, interfaith or interracial marriage, immodest dress, the history of vaccines, and evolution.[29] The line between

---

[24] Sotomayor's dissent 15, citing *Kennedy v. Bremerton School District* (*supra* note 5) and *Town of Greece v. Galloway* 572 U.S. 565, 589 (2014).
[25] *Id.* at 14.
[26] *Id.* at 2.
[27] *Id.* at 27–28, 34, 36.
[28] *Id.* at 19.
[29] *Id.* at 22–23, 27; Sotomayor, oral argument transcript at 20, 29.

exposure and impermissible burdens on free exercise seems blurred: Would a photograph of a teacher's gay partner or spouse displayed on their desk have to be removed? School officials who seek to encourage civility and respect for LGBTQ+ and others who have faced discrimination will face high administrative burdens and little sympathy from a Court when challenged by conservative religious adherents.

CHAPTER 13

Catholic Charities Bureau, Inc. v. Wisconsin: A Blip on the Roberts Court's Path to Narrowing the Establishment Clause and Expanding Free Exercise

George Thomas

Unlike the other Supreme Court cases decided in 2025 that took up questions under the Constitution's religion clauses, *Catholic Charities Bureau, Inc. v. Wisconsin Labor and Industry Review Commission* is situated in long-standing jurisprudence.[1] In a unanimous opinion by Justice Sonia Sotomayor, the Court held that the First Amendment "mandates government neutrality between religions" and when a law appears to privilege particular religious understandings it must be subject to the Court's highest level of scrutiny, that is, "strict scrutiny." While the Court's opinion was nominally based on the Establishment Clause, its greatest impact is

---

[1] *Catholic Charities Bureau, Inc. v. Wisconsin Labor and Industry Review Commission* 605 U.S. ___ (2025).

G. Thomas (✉)
Claremont McKenna College, Claremont, CA, USA
e-mail: gthomas@cmc.edu

likely to be in the realm of free exercise. Indeed, while on the surface *Catholic Charities* broke no new doctrinal ground, it reinforces the Roberts Court's expansive reading of free exercise rights even if it does so, ironically, by offering a fairly traditional understanding of the Establishment Clause. In this, *Catholic Charities* sits uneasily alongside the Roberts Court's recent cases that have narrowed the scope of the Establishment Clause, but it is consistent with the Roberts Court's favorable treatment of religious claims under the Free Exercise Clause, where it has been particularly sympathetic to conservative religious claims.[2]

The Facts and Constitutional Argument

Under Wisconsin law, religious employers are exempt from paying taxes into the state's unemployment compensation system. The exemption not only extended to ministers and members of a religious order engaged in explicitly religious duties, but it also applied to non-profit organizations if they (1) were run by a church and (2) if they were "operated primarily for religious purposes."[3] As a non-profit charity, Catholic Charities Bureau sought such an exemption. After a lengthy back and forth with the state, it was ultimately denied the exemption by the Wisconsin Supreme Court. While the Wisconsin Supreme Court agreed that Catholic Charities and the various organizations under it were controlled by the Catholic Church, it held that the charitable work it engaged in was primarily secular, rather than religious, so it did not qualify for the exemption.

Wisconsin defended this distinction between religious and secular purposes within religious organizations as crucial to maintaining the state's unemployment compensation system, while at the same time giving religious institutions autonomy over their genuinely religious activities. Based on earlier Supreme Court decisions, Wisconsin argued that religious employers should have complete discretion over employees who are engaged in religious activities as such. Religious institutions could thus fire an employee for religious reasons, acting as the sole judge of whether the employee was correctly following religious doctrine, without being

---

[2] Lee Epstein and Eric Posner, "The Roberts Court and the Transformation of Constitutional Protections for Religion: A Statistical Portrait" *Supreme Court Review* 2021 (Chicago: University of Chicago Press, 2022), 325. There are cases coming up through the court system asking for religious exemptions from stricter abortion laws, which will test if the Roberts Court will be as sympathetic to more liberal free exercise claims.

[3] *Catholic Charities* at 2 (slip opinion).

subject to employment discrimination claims. On the other hand, where the religious institution was operating a secular charitable undertaking, rules about employment and contributions to unemployment should apply.

Wisconsin argued that it was following the logic the Court had set out regarding ministerial exemptions, which insulated religious organizations from employment laws when the employee, like a minister, was fulfilling religious functions, but did not provide such insulation with respect to employees engaged in secular activities. As Wisconsin argued, this was consistent with the Court's recent cases such as *Hosanna-Tabor Evangelical Lutheran Church and School* (2012). Wisconsin also noted that its justifications for its unemployment exemptions scheme followed the logic of earlier Supreme Court precedent beginning with *Lemon v. Kurtzman* in 1971, which warned against laws that unnecessarily "entangled" the state with religious institutions.[4] By providing for religious exemptions in its unemployment scheme, Wisconsin said, the state gave wide birth to free exercise and avoided any Establishment Clause issues.

The Wisconsin Supreme Court held that under Wisconsin law a "religious purpose" required the charity to be engaged in proselytizing or providing charity exclusively to members of the religion. While Wisconsin recognized that Catholic Charities was religiously controlled, it nevertheless deemed it ineligible for the exemption because it did not "attempt to imbue program participants with the Catholic faith, supply religious materials to program participants or employees, or limit their charitable services to members of the Catholic Church."[5] According to the Wisconsin Supreme Court, Catholic Charities was a religious organization effectively engaged in secular charitable work. Yet Catholic Charities insisted that it was following Catholic religious teaching, which commanded that it extend charity to all regardless of their religious faith and that it not proselytize while providing charity. In short, the behavior that disqualified it for a religious exemption was driven by religious belief. Because Wisconsin was defining religious purpose as requiring proselytization, it was impermissibly burdening Catholic Charities free exercise rights.

The central dispute turned on how to define when a religious organization was engaged in a "religious purpose." Both sides framed their arguments in terms of the Free Exercise Clause, with Catholic Charities

---

[4] The Roberts Court formally overturned *Lemon* in *Kennedy v. Bremerton School District* (2022).
[5] *Catholic Charities* at 10.

claiming that the requirement to contribute to the state's unemployment compensation fund was a "substantial burden" on their religious practices, while Wisconsin argued that no religious practice was being burdened.

The Court's Opinion and Supreme Court Precedent

The Supreme Court agreed with Catholic Charities. But rather than focusing on the Free Exercise Clause, the Court ruled that the state appeared to favor some religions over others in violation of the Establishment Clause. As Justice Sotomayor argued, the Court's precedents made clear that states must be neutral with regard to different religions: "denominational neutrality bars States from passing laws that 'aid or oppose particular religions'" or laws that "interfere in the 'competition between sects.'"[6] Sotomayor rested this argument on long-standing Establishment Clause jurisprudence. Indeed, Sotomayor cited precedents such as *Epperson v. Arkansas* (1968), *Zorach v. Clauson* (1952), and *School District of Abington Township v. Schempp* (1963) that articulated a fairly strict separation of church and state—much stricter, in fact, then the version that the Roberts Court's recent opinions have embraced. Yet these cases also insisted that violating the principle of neutrality between different religious denominations not only violated the Establishment Clause but also implicated the "vitality" of the Free Exercise Clause. When government actions appear to "favor certain religions," it coveys to members of other faiths that "they are not full members of the political community." In this way, the Establishment Clause's insistence on neutrality aids the full realization of "true religious liberty," which requires the government to "refrain from 'favoritism among sects'."[7]

The trouble, Sotomayor argued, was that while Wisconsin was attempting to avoid engaging in determinations about the particulars of faith when it came to unemployment law, it created a problem by using essentially religious criteria to determine whether a religious charity was engaged in secular or religious activity. In interpreting its law to require that the charitable organization be both religious and engaged in some form of preaching about its religion for the charitable activity to count as religious under the terms of the exemption, the Wisconsin Supreme Court was

---

[6] *Catholic Charities* at 8.
[7] *Catholic Charities* at 8.

"differentiating between religions based on theological practices."[8] Two religious charities could be engaged in the same charitable work, but if one of the two preached while doing it and the other one did not (for theological reasons), then the first charity would be entitled to the exemption, while the second would not.[9] In drawing a distinction between what counts as religious activity based on religious understandings, Wisconsin was violating the principle of religious neutrality.

It is important to note that *Catholic Charities* does not hold that religious exemptions are required under the Free Exercise Clause. Indeed, the opinion rests on the Establishment Clause, only holding that when a state does grant particular privileges to religious organizations under its laws, it must do so in a neutral manner. Nor does the Court hold that any religiously motivated activity would be entitled to an exemption if a state grants religious exemptions under its law. The holding is much narrower than that.[10] It is in fact consistent with *Employment Division v. Smith* (1991), authored by the conservative judicial icon Antonin Scalia, which held that the Free Exercise Clause did not require religious exemptions against an otherwise valid law.[11] Under *Smith*, if a law is neutral between religions, applied in a neutral manner, and serves a legitimate secular purpose, it is consistent with the commands of free exercise. The Court could have found that Wisconsin's Supreme Court opinion applied the law in a non-neutral manner insofar as it turned to religious criteria to determine if the activity in question was for religious purposes. Yet such an opinion would have reaffirmed *Smith*, which the Roberts Court has been walking away from, often over the dissenting opinions of the liberal justices, while the conservative justices Alito, Gorsuch, and Thomas have emphatically insisted that *Smith* is wrongly decided and should be formally overturned.[12] By relying on the Establishment Clause's command that any

---

[8] *Catholic Charities* at 10.

[9] Justice Ketanji Jackson's concurrence argues that the proper question is what activity the organization is engaged in, not what its purpose is, but she agreed that the Wisconsin Supreme Court's understanding of religious purpose was not neutral.

[10] The key here is that Wisconsin law required that the charity be controlled by a church and engaged in a religious purpose. The Court's holding would not apply to a secular charity driven by a religious purpose, let alone to a commercial institution driven by a religious purpose.

[11] Employment Division, Department of Human Resources of Oregon v. Smith 494 U.S. 872 (1990).

[12] Burwell v. Hobby Lobby 573 U.S. 682 (2014) (J. Ginsburg dissenting joined by Breyer, Kagan, and Sotomayor); Fulton v. City of Philadelphia 593 U.S. ___ (2021) (J. Alito concurring joined by Gorsuch and Thomas).

benefits given to religious organizations be given on a non-preferential basis, the Court avoided this Free Exercise Clause battle. In doing so, Sotomayor's opinion was able to bring liberal and conservative justices together around the principle of neutrality between religions. But this is an uneasy alliance that rests on the particulars of this case and is largely out of step with the Roberts Court's opinions on church and state.[13]

The reach of *Catholic Charities* is likely to be limited as it masks these profound disagreements. The other cases taking up the Constitution's religion clauses this term are more representative of the Roberts Court's trajectory on issues of church and state. In *Mahmoud v. Taylor*, the Court offered a sweeping reading of free exercise, insisting the Constitution exempted religious believers against exposure to ideas that clash with their religious beliefs in the public school system even when such laws are neutral in their aim to foster civic understandings and tolerance. In this case, Justice Alito's opinion put a clear emphasis on the religious motivation of parents. Sotomayor dissented in *Mahmoud*, arguing that the Court "cast aside longstanding precedent" to invent "a constitutional right to avoid exposure to 'subtle' themes 'contrary to the religious principles' that parents wish to instill in their children."[14] And while the Court divided 4–4 in *Oklahoma State Wide Charter School Board v. Drummond*, allowing the lower court opinion to stand, there is now an active argument on the Court that states can directly fund religious educational institutions without violating the Establishment Clause. Indeed, it appears there are four justices who think declining to fund sectarian institutions if the state funds private secular institutions violates the Free Exercise Clause.

CATHOLIC CHARITIES AND THE ROBERTS COURT'S CHURCH–STATE JURISPRUDENCE

Drawing on jurisprudence from the middle years of the twentieth century, *Catholic Charities* is out of line with the Roberts Court's more recent precedents, even while it can be situated within the Rehnquist Court's

---

[13] It could well be that Justice Sotomayor seized on this as a way to bring the Court together and attempt to shape its Establishment Clause jurisprudence. It may well be that Justices Breyer and Kagan did this in earlier free exercises cases as well.

[14] *Mahmoud v. Taylor* 606 U.S. ____ (2025) (Sotomayor dissenting at 1, joined by Kagan and Jackson).

cases that insisted upon neutrality as the guiding point in its Establishment Clause decisions. In fact, Sotomayor's opinion in *Catholic Charities*, as well as her dissent in *Mahmoud*, has common ground with precedents from the Rehnquist Court, which highlights that the conservatives on the Roberts Court have been engaged in narrowing the Establishment Clause while expanding the Free Exercise Clause.

In *Espinoza v. Montana* (2020), the Roberts Court insisted that state aid—if available to secular institutions—not only may but *must* be available to sectarian institutions to avoid religious discrimination under the Free Exercise Clause. In *Espinoza* the Court's opinion quickly dismissed questions about the Establishment Clause and then found that a provision of Montana's constitution prohibiting aid to religious educational institutions, which had existed for well over a century, violated the Free Exercise Clause. This was a novel departure, as States had long declined to fund explicitly religious education with no free exercise issues raised. Even as the Rehnquist Court walked back the Court's earlier and stricter forms of separation under the Establishment Clause, it did not hold that states must fund religious instruction or violate the Free Exercise Clause.[15] Yet that is precisely what the Roberts Court commanded in *Espinoza* and *Carson v. Makin* (2022).

This shift is most visible in Justice Thomas's concurring opinion in *Catholic Charities*. In short, Thomas argued that while Wisconsin was attempting to adhere to earlier Court precedents regarding the Establishment Clause, those understandings had not only been overturned but were in violation of free exercise rights. Thomas's interpretation of free exercise is a profound break with Scalia's *Smith* decision; yet it symbolizes the vanguard of the Roberts Court's conservative-wing, which is eager to dismantle Scalia's free exercise jurisprudence.

The Political Landscape

The Roberts Court reflects the profound changes in the political landscape over the last two decades. Before the Roberts Court, liberals and conservatives were on both sides of free exercise questions. It was, after all, Justice William Brennan, a liberal lion from the Warren Court, who wrote the first opinion insisting that free exercise requires exemptions for

---

[15] *Locke v. Davey* 540 U.S. 712 (2004) (though Thomas and Scalia dissented on this point).

religious practices against an otherwise valid law.[16] And it was the conservative originalist, Justice Scalia, who rejected that argument and insisted that a neutral law, neutrally applied was perfectly consistent with the constitutional command to protect free exercise.[17] Reacting against Scalia's *Smith* opinion when it was handed down in 1990, which had rejected an exemptions claim from members of the Native American Church, both Democrats and Republicans championed the Religious Freedom Restoration Act (RFRA), which sought to return the Court to earlier precedents—though, in truth, there were precedents on both sides of the issue, just as there were once liberals and conservatives on both sides of the issue. That has changed. Senator Chuck Schumer (D-NY) sponsored RFRA back when he was a member of the House of Representatives and the bill was signed into law by President Bill Clinton. Today, Schumer, like most Democrats, opposes the act he once saw as protecting religious minorities.[18]

In contrast, most Republicans insist on a robust understanding of free exercise that requires exemptions in all kinds of cases that go far beyond precedents like *Sherbert v. Verner* (1963) and *Wisconsin v. Yoder* (1972). They would extend religious exemptions to private businesses engaged in routine commercial activity simply because their owners have religious beliefs. So, for instance, a baker whose business is open to all comers does not have to bake a cake for a same-sex couple in celebration of their union if he happens to think homosexuality is immoral for religious reasons.[19] Religious claims, especially the claims of mainstream Christian religions, regularly win on the Roberts Court, particularly in comparison to past Courts. According to one study, religious claims have won on the Roberts Court 83% of the time (and it is particularly solicitous of conservative religious claims). In comparison, religious claims prevailed on the Rehnquist Court, the next most favorable Court, 58% of the time.[20]

---

[16] *Sherbert v. Verner* 374 U.S. 398 (1963).

[17] *Employment Division, Department of Human Resources of Oregon v. Smith* 494 U.S. 872 (1990).

[18] John S. Blattner, "Render unto Caesar: How Misunderstanding a Century of Free Exercise Jurisprudence Forged and Then Fractured the RFRA Coalition" (2017) CMC Senior Thesis, 1575, 13.

[19] *Masterpiece Cakeshop, Ltd. v. Colorado Civil Rights Commission* (2018).

[20] Lee Epstein and Eric Posner, "The Roberts Court and the Transformation of Constitutional Protections for Religion: A Statistical Portrait" *Supreme Court Review* 2021 (Chicago: University of Chicago Press, 2022), 325.

Given the Roberts Court's disposition, we can expect more expansive claims about free exercise, particularly given that some Republicans insist that traditional religion, especially traditional Christian understandings, are under siege in an increasingly secular society. To wit: the Becket Fund for Religious Liberty, which litigates for free exercise accommodations for all religions, has won all eight cases it brought to the Supreme Court since 2012 (including *Mahmoud*).[21] While Becket's cases include victories for the accommodations understanding for minority religions and have included unanimous decisions from the Court, they are nonetheless telling of the broader picture. In the eight cases they brought that were squarely about religious liberty, a Democratic administration supported one—a case about a Muslim inmate asking for an accommodation that would allow him to grow a beard consistent with his religious belief. He prevailed in a unanimous Court opinion. In the three other cases where a Democratic administration could have supported the claim for a religious exemption, it defended federal law against the exemptions claim (with a mainstream Christian asking for the exemption in each case). Similarly, a Republican administration supported every claim favoring a religious exemption (while all four were for a mainstream Christian religion, one claim included Muslims). While this is only a sketch, it reflects the division between the political parties on religious liberty and its implications for church and state more broadly.

Returning to *Catholic Charities*, it is not at all surprising that the Trump administration supported Catholic Charities' claim before the Court. We can expect this trend to continue, as the Roberts Court solidifies an expansive understanding of free exercise driven by a narrowing of the Establishment Clause where *Catholic Charities* is a blip in the road.

---

[21] Figures from the Becket Fund's website: https://becketfund.org.

CHAPTER 14

U.S. v. Skrmetti: Rejecting a Challenge to Bans on Gender-Affirming Care Without Resolving Key Questions About the Rights of Transgender Individuals

Susan Etta Keller

In U.S. v. Skrmetti, the Supreme Court upheld a statute that denied gender-affirming care to transgender youth and rejected the claim that the classifications made in the statute required the application of intermediate scrutiny under the Equal Protection clause. The majority avoided addressing some of the more searching questions regarding the rights of transgender individuals by engaging in logical contortions. At the same time, the majority and the concurring justices demonstrate a much greater sympathy to the concerns of state legislators than to the circumstances of the affected young people or the experts that support them.

The case arrives at the seeming crest of a years-long backlash of legislative actions targeting transgender individuals following the Court's decision in *Bostock v. Clayton County*, which held that discrimination on the basis of either sexual orientation or transgender status was a form of sex

S. E. Keller (✉)
Western State College of Law, Irvine, CA, USA
e-mail: Skeller@wsu.law.edu

discrimination under Title VII.[1] While federal courts initially struck down such legislation, including bathroom bans, sports bans, and bans on gender-affirming care, recent decisions, as well as public opinion, have moved toward upholding these restrictions. Although the Court in *Skrmetti* leaves *Bostock* untouched, its approach is quite different from that taken in the earlier case.

Some procedural history is necessary to explain how the *Skrmetti* Court came to focus exclusively on Equal Protection. Initially brought as *L.W. v. Skrmetti* on behalf of private patients and their parents, the case raised multiple claims.[2] The District Court found that with respect to its bans on puberty blockers and cross-sex hormones, the statute violated both the Equal Protection rights of the minor patients because it discriminated against them on the basis of sex and transgender status, and also the Substantive Due Process rights of their parents to "direct the medical care of their children."[3] The Sixth Circuit appeal consolidated the Tennessee case with a similar one from Kentucky, and the United States intervened solely on the issue of Equal Protection.[4] After the Sixth Circuit rejected both the Equal Protection and Substantive Due Process challenges, the Supreme Court granted the *certiorari* petition of the United States but not that of the private petitioners, thus limiting the question before it to the Equal Protection challenge.[5] As a result, the only legal question before the Court was whether the classifications in the Tennessee statute triggered intermediate scrutiny as the District Court had found.

---

[1] *Bostock v. Clayton Cnty.*, 140 S. Ct. 1731 (2020); *See generally*, Susan Etta Keller, *Doing Things with the Language of Law and Gender: Using Speech Act Theory to Understand the Meaning and Effect of the Gender Identity Backlash*, 24 Nev. L. J. 413 (2024).

[2] *L.W. v. Skrmetti*, 83 F. 4th 460, 469 (6th Cir. 2023) (name assigned to one minor plaintiff was L.W., Jonathan Skrmetti is the Attorney General of Tennessee).

[3] *Id.*

[4] *Id.* at 470 (US intervening as they are entitled to do under federal statutory law when a case includes an Equal Protection challenge that raises questions of "general public importance").

[5] 144 S. Ct. 267 (2024) After oral argument and the change of administrations in January 2025, the United States withdrew its support for the Equal Protection challenge, but the case proceeded anyway. *See U.S. v. Skrmetti*, No. 23-477, slip op. at 8, n.1 (U.S. June 18, 2025).

The most significant upshot of how the case was limited is that the Supreme Court did not address the issue of Substantive Due Process rights, which remains a basis for parents of transgender youth to challenge similar statutes in other circuits.[6] But the ways in which the majority chose to frame the question also result in a more limited holding that puts off for future cases the more fundamental question of whether direct discrimination against transgender individuals triggers heightened scrutiny.

The Majority's Logic

By rejecting the petitioners' argument that intermediate scrutiny ought to apply, the majority affirms the Sixth Circuit decision that the statute does not violate the Equal Protection clause, because it passes muster under the lower rational basis test. The majority opinion, authored by Chief Justice Roberts, arrives at this conclusion by arguing that the statute does not discriminate on the basis of sex and that it also does not discriminate on the basis of transgender status.

Rather than classifying on the basis of sex, the majority argues that the statute classifies instead on the basis of age and "medical use." The medical use referred to is the use of puberty blockers and hormones to treat gender dysphoria, and related conditions in minors, as opposed to other conditions for which the same medications remain available.[7] As the majority notes, the reference to "sex" in the statute is not alone conclusive that it involves sex discrimination.[8] Harder to refute is the contention that by limiting the conditions for which these medications can be used to those that afflict only transgender youth, the statute "prohibits certain treatments for minors of one sex while allowing those same treatments for minors of the opposite sex."[9] As dissenting Justice Sotomayor puts it: "Male (but not female) adolescents can receive medicines that help them

---

[6] *See* Transcript of Oral Argument at 142 (10–15), U.S. v. Skrmetti, 145 S. Ct. 1816 (2025) (No. 23-477) (Justice Barrett's comments).
[7] *Skrmetti*, slip op. at 9.
[8] *Id.* at 10.
[9] *Id.* at 11.

look like boys, and female (but not male) adolescents can receive medicines that help them look like girls."[10]

The majority argues that because the statute outlaws access by minors of both sexes to treatments for only a certain set of medical conditions and not others, it does not discriminate on the basis of sex.[11] Justice Sotomayor points out that a similar argument was once made to justify anti-miscegenation statutes: "A prohibition on interracial marriage, for example, allows no person to marry someone outside of her race, while allowing persons of any race to marry within their races."[12] Of course, *Loving v. Virginia* rejected this logic and found that a statute that prohibited both black and white people from marrying people outside their race still classified on the basis of race and was subject to strict scrutiny.[13] While acknowledging that under *Loving*, a statute cannot mask a suspect class classification by using "abstract terms," the majority denies that is occurring with the statute under review. In refutation it states:

> Under SB1, no minor may be administered puberty blockers or hormones to treat gender dysphoria, gender identity disorder, or gender incongruence; minors of any sex may be administered puberty blockers or hormones for other purposes.[14]

But this explanation reads to the dissent as having the same logic as the argument rejected in *Loving*. "The problem with the majority's argument," Justice Sotomayor explains, "is that the very 'medical purpose' SB1 prohibits is defined by reference to the patient's sex."[15] The statute "renders every treatment decision it regulates dependent on two things: a minor's sex identified at birth, and the consistency of the requested treatment with that sex."[16]

The Court's earlier decision in *Bostock* provides another obstacle the majority quickly dismisses. Leaving that decision undisturbed, the majority does not even decide the question that has bedeviled lower courts

---

[10] *U.S. v. Skrmetti*, No. 23-477, slip op. at 2 (Sotomayor, J., dissenting) (U.S. June 18, 2025).
[11] *Id.* at 12–13.
[12] *Id.* at 18 (Sotomayor, J., dissenting).
[13] *Loving v. Virginia*, 388 U.S. 1, 11 (1967).
[14] *Skrmetti*, slip op. at 13.
[15] *Id.* at 16 (Sotomayor, J., dissenting).
[16] *Id.* at 17 (Sotomayor, J., dissenting).

regarding its applicability to questions outside the Title VII context such as Equal Protection law. Rather, the majority claims that the discrimination occasioned by the Tennessee statute is different. Whereas in *Bostock*, an employer who was as likely to fire transgender men as transgender women because of their transgender status was still liable for sex discrimination because the sex assigned at birth was a but-for cause of the discrimination, the majority in *Skrmetti* argues that sex is not the but-for cause for the treatment ban. That's because a transgender individual who suffered from one of the approved bases for use of puberty blockers or hormone treatments (such as precocious puberty) could still access that care. But as Justice Sotomayor points out, *Bostock* did not require that sex be the only basis for a decision to count as sex discrimination: if "sex is 'one but-for cause of that decision,' the employer discriminates on the basis of sex."[17]

Finally, the majority avoids the question of whether transgender status itself might qualify as a "quasi-suspect" class warranting intermediate scrutiny by arguing that the relevant statute does not discriminate on that basis either, again because of the possibility that a transgender individual might qualify for treatment based on a diagnosis unrelated to gender dysphoria. Both concurring Justices Alito and Barrett part ways with the majority on this point, each concluding that the statute does discriminate on that basis but that transgender status does not qualify for heightened scrutiny. Justice Alito argues primarily that the class lacks an "immutable" characteristic and is too "amorphous" and "diverse" to qualify,[18] while Justice Barrett questions whether transgender individuals have faced a history of "*de jure*" discrimination sufficient to qualify,[19] despite the detailed history Justice Sotomayor offers of such discrimination.[20] It is hard to see how this factor could any longer be in dispute in light of the multiple Executive Orders in early 2025 directly targeting transgender individuals.[21]

The qualities of the majority opinion that make its logic so hard to follow are directly related to the questions it avoids. Because the Court says

---

[17] *Id*. at 20 (Sotomayor, J., dissenting).
[18] *U.S. v. Skrmetti*, No. 23-477, slip op. at 20–21 (Alito, J., concurring) (U.S. June 18, 2025).
[19] *U.S. v. Skrmetti*, No. 23-477, slip op. at 10 (Barrett, J., concurring) (U.S. June 18, 2025).
[20] *Id*. at 25–26 (Sotomayor, J., dissenting).
[21] Justice Barrett seems to recognize the potential for a showing of such de jure discrimination but maintains that the showing was not made in the parties' briefs. *Id*. at 11, n. 5 (Barrett, J., concurring).

that the statutes discriminate only on the basis of age and diagnostic category, circumstances of discrimination in which those bases do not apply might still be susceptible to claims of sex discrimination. By leaving *Bostock* in place, constitutional claims based on analogies to that case remain available. Finally, because the Court does not directly confront the question of whether transgender status itself might trigger heightened scrutiny, it leaves open the possibility of a successful constitutional claim in another context that involves more explicit discrimination on the basis of that status.

Attitude Toward Experts

Because the only legal question before the Court was the level of scrutiny required, the comparative merits of medical opinion regarding the risks and benefits of gender-affirming care for minors was beside the point.[22] Nevertheless, the majority opinion pits experts on "both sides" against each other to create a controversy sufficient to justify the deference it assigns the state legislature as arbiter of this controversy. Although the substantial majority of major American medical associations approve of the use of gender-affirming care in appropriate and carefully screened cases,[23] the majority's effort to identify weighty arguments on the other side is a necessary pre-condition to its assertion that the absence of consensus means legislatures ought to be free to either support or limit such care. For example, the majority identifies the very fact that half the states impose such bans as illustrating a valid difference of opinion.[24] Studies from European countries that have urged greater caution in those countries' oversight of gender-affirming care, but that have not caused those countries to outright ban such care,[25] are further used to add weight to the other side of the ledger, suggesting the medical science is "evolving" and the subject of "fierce scientific and policy debates"[26] rather than well-settled. Although not related to the legal argument the Court advances to reject heightened scrutiny, the majority relies on these statements rhetorically to ask the reading public to accept its hands-off approach: "The

---

[22] *Id.* at 29 (Sotomayor, J., dissenting) ("Infusing that antecedent legal question with a host of evidence relevant only to the subsequent application of judicial scrutiny…simply puts the cart before the horse").

[23] *Id.* at 5 (Sotomayor, J., dissenting).

[24] *Id.* at 3.

[25] *Id.* at 29 (Sotomayor, J., dissenting).

[26] *Id.* at 24.

Equal Protection Clause does not resolve these disagreements. Nor does it afford us license to decide them as we see best."[27]

The concurrence of Justice Thomas, which goes beyond the majority's approach to dismiss the relevance of experts entirely, is a stunning harbinger of an approach he or other justices might take to future legislation or administrative action that defies received scientific or medical wisdom. Contemptuously referring to the major medical organizations that were *amici curiae* or cited as authorities in the plaintiffs' briefs as "so-called experts"[28] and "self-proclaimed experts,"[29] Thomas dismisses their perspectives as unworthy of consideration. Not satisfied with undermining the views of experts in general, Thomas seeks to question more specifically the integrity of those experts with whom he disagrees.[30] He suggests that medical experts supporting gender-affirming care, but not those taking the opposite view, "have surreptitiously compromised their medical recommendations to achieve political ends,"[31] explicitly suggesting that to defer to their view would be equivalent to the deference paid to eugenicists in the early twentieth century.[32] In this respect he joins the Trump administration and the Attorney General of Texas in creating visceral associations in the public mind between the modern provision of gender-affirming care and various unrelated atrocities.[33]

In contrast to the experts, Thomas, like the majority, exalts the legislative process itself. To take the views of medical organizations into account, he states, "would permit elite sentiment to distort and stifle democratic

---

[27] *Id.*
[28] *U.S. v. Skrmetti*, No. 23-477, slip op. at 5 (Thomas, J. concurring) (U.S. June 18, 2025).
[29] *Id.* at 7 (Thomas, J., concurring). He doubles down on the disdain by placing scare quotes around the phrase "major medical organizations."
[30] *See Id.* at 6 n. 5 (Sotomayor, J., dissenting) (pointing out that despite his declaration that expertise is irrelevant, Thomas cannot refrain from promoting the views of experts whose viewpoint he favors).
[31] *Id.* at 23 (Thomas, J., concurring).
[32] *Id.* at 7 (Thomas, J., concurring).
[33] Memorandum from the Attorney General of the U.S. For Select Component Heads, Preventing the Mutilation of American Children (April 22, 2025) (https://www.justice.gov/ag/media/1402396/dl) (Pam Bondi directive associating gender-affirming care with Female Genital Mutilation); Tex. Att'y Gen. Op. No. KP-0401, Whether certain medical procedures performed on children constitute child abuse (RQ-0426-KP) (February 18, 2022) (https://texasattorneygeneral.gov/sites/default/files/global/KP-0401.pdf) (Kenneth Paxton letter associating gender-affirming care with forced sterilization programs).

debate under the guise of scientific judgment."[34] Here, evidence-based opinion is rendered a masquerade ("under the guise") and demoted to a mere "elite sentiment." That sentiment is contrasted with "the wisdom, fairness, or logic of legislative choices."[35]

By concluding that the disputes in the scientific evidence require deference to the legislature, the arguments of the majority and of Thomas once again bring to mind an analogy with *Loving v. Virginia*. In that case, the Court rejected the state's claim that disputed scientific evidence about the supposed harms of interracial marriage meant that the Court "should defer to the wisdom of the state legislature in adopting its policy of discouraging interracial marriages."[36]

What's at Stake

For all the solicitude the majority and concurring justices offer for the democratic process and the legislature, there is little consideration of the impact of the decision on the actual lives of transgender young people. Transgender youth exist within the majority's opinion only as fictive patients within hypotheticals. Statutory language that might otherwise stand out as evidence of animus is painted instead by the majority as care. The statute's findings describing the state's purpose as "encouraging minors to appreciate their sex" and avoiding treatments "that might encourage minors to become disdainful of their sex" had persuaded both plaintiffs and the dissenters that the statute was motivated by a purpose to enforce sex stereotyping.[37] The majority reads the same language as reflecting the state's "concerns" about negative effects from the treatment against which the legislators sought to "protect" the children.[38] In this respect there is great sympathy expressed for the efforts of these legislatures to craft appropriate policy but nary a word for the perspective of the teens affected by it.

It is left to Justice Sotomayor to cast the human stakes in high relief. As she notes, access to gender-affirming care is a matter of "life and death" for teens suffering from a condition, gender dysphoria, associated with a

---

[34] *Id.* at 6 (Thomas, J., concurring).
[35] *Id.* at 5 (Thomas, J., concurring).
[36] *Loving*, 388 U.S. at 8.
[37] *Skrmetti*, slip op. at 15.
[38] *Id.*

high rate of suicide.[39] She provides the stories of the real teenagers who were the plaintiffs in the Tennessee case, documenting their suffering and the relief they obtained from care they are now denied.[40]

What's Next

As discussed above, the focus in the Supreme Court on Equal Protection means that Substantive Due Process rights remain a basis for parents of transgender youth to challenge similar statutes in other circuits. Also, nothing in the Supreme Court decision directly affects the rights to gender-affirming care in the remaining states that have not instituted bans. The president's executive order purporting to apply a similar ban nationwide by withholding federal funds[41] has been enjoined in part on the basis that it violates the separation of powers.[42]

Finally, and most significantly, the Court's holding that the state ban on gender-affirming care discriminates neither on the basis of sex nor on the basis of transgender status further limits the scope of *Skrmetti*. While there is plenty to question about the logic of both prongs of this holding, its effect is to leave open avenues for possible future relief for claims of discrimination on either of these bases, for example, in a case that more directly classifies on the basis of transgender status. Perhaps the majority fashioned its awkward reasoning in order to avoid confronting those questions. It is likely, however, that the cases regarding transgender athletes, which the Court has taken up for the October 2025 term,[43] will serve as vehicles for addressing more directly the level of scrutiny required for cases discriminating against transgender individuals.

---

[39] *Id.* at 4–5 (Sotomayor, J., dissenting).

[40] *Id.* at 7–8 (Sotomayor, J., dissenting).

[41] Exec. Order No. 14,187, 90 Fed. Reg. 8771 (Jan. 28, 2025) (titled "Protecting Children from Chemical and Surgical Mutilation").

[42] *PFLAG v. Trump*, No. 25-337-BAH, slip op. at 45 (D. Md. March 4, 2025). However, whether that injunction will ultimately be upheld is cast in some doubt by the outcome of Trump v. CASA.

[43] Kelsey Dallas, *Supreme Court takes up cases on transgender athletes*, SCOTUSblog (Jul. 3, 2025, 11:08 AM), [https://www.scotusblog.com/2025/07/supreme-court-takes-up-cases-on-transgender-athletes/].

CHAPTER 15

Free Speech Coalition, Inc. v. Paxton: Sexually Explicit Speech Online and Age Verification

Eric T. Kasper

The internet has led to revolutionary changes in commerce, political discourse, and media communications. It has also led to the proliferation of pornography online. This has resulted not only in consenting adults having greater access to produce and view sexually themed expression; it has also raised serious concerns about children's access to pornographic materials. These competing concerns of protecting First Amendment rights for adults and safeguarding children from harm were the matters litigated in *Free Speech Coalition, Inc. v. Paxton*. In that case, the US Supreme Court upheld a Texas law that requires commercial websites publishing sexual material harmful to minors to verify that users are at least 18 years of age.

THE LEGAL CONTEXT

In 1991, the hip-hop group Salt-N-Pepa released a commercially successful single, titled "Let's Talk About Sex." Indeed, people have been talking about sex since time immemorial. In *Roth v. United States* (1957), the US Supreme Court stated that the "portrayal of sex, e.g., in art, literature and

E. T. Kasper (✉)
University of Wisconsin-Eau Claire, Eau Claire, WI, USA
e-mail: kasperet@uwec.edu

© The Author(s), under exclusive license to Springer Nature Switzerland AG 2026
H. Schweber (ed.), *SCOTUS 2025*,
https://doi.org/10.1007/978-3-032-10231-7_15

scientific works, is not itself sufficient reason to deny material the constitutional protection of freedom of speech and press," because "[s]ex, a great and mysterious motive force in human life, has indisputably been a subject of absorbing interest to mankind through the ages."[1]

Nevertheless, the Court also held in *Roth* that if sexually explicit material is obscene, it is not protected by the First Amendment. The Court struggled to consistently articulate a definition for obscenity until *Miller v. California* (1973), announcing in that case a test that remains the standard for defining obscenity today: "(a) whether the average person, applying contemporary community standards would find that the work, taken as a whole, appeals to the prurient interest; (b) whether the work depicts or describes, in a patently offensive way, sexual conduct specifically defined by the applicable state law; and (c) whether the work, taken as a whole, lacks serious literary, artistic, political, or scientific value."[2] Although obscenity prosecutions have tapered off in recent years because of a shift in contemporary community standards regarding pornography,[3] obscenity remains categorically excluded from First Amendment protection.[4]

But even if non-obscene sexually explicit expression has some First Amendment coverage, that does *not* mean that one has a right to display, engage in, or consume that speech whenever, wherever, and however one likes. For instance, in *Ginsberg v. New York* (1968), the Supreme Court upheld a state law prohibiting the sale of pornographic magazines to minors under the age of 17, even when the sexually explicit material at issue was *not* obscene for adults, on the grounds that the material was harmful to minors.[5] Still, the Court has been clear for decades that the government may not "reduce the adult population ... to reading only what is fit for children," by "quarantining the general reading public against books not too rugged for grown men and women in order to shield juvenile innocence," as "this is to burn the house to roast the pig."[6]

How, then, does the First Amendment balance free expression rights for adults and governmental power to protect children from harm? Like speech on other topics, sexually explicit expression is subject to time,

---

[1] Roth v. United States, 354 U.S. 476, 487 (1957).
[2] Miller v. California, 413 U.S. 15, 24 (1973) (internal citations and quotations omitted).
[3] *See* Kendra Albert, "Imagine A Community: Obscenity's History and Moderating Speech Online," *Yale Journal of Law and Technology* (2023) 25 59–75, 66.
[4] *See* Counterman v. Colorado, 600 U.S. 66, 73 (2023).
[5] Ginsberg v. New York, 390 U.S. 629, 631, 634–35, 643, 645 (1968).
[6] Butler v. Michigan, 352 U.S. 380, 383 (1957).

place, and manner regulations. When the government regulates speech, the First Amendment test will vary based on the type of regulation at issue. If the government restricts speech based on its content (meaning that certain topics are targeted), those laws "are presumptively unconstitutional," and subject to strict scrutiny.[7] If a law is subject to this very demanding test, then the law "[1] must be the least restrictive means [2] of achieving a compelling state interest."[8] This test is very difficult for a law to pass because, under the First Amendment, "our people are guaranteed the right to express any thought, free from government censorship. The essence of this forbidden censorship is content control."[9]

Conversely, some speech regulations are content neutral, in that they apply equally to all speech, regardless of a speaker's topic or point of view. This would include limits on the decibel level of expression or prohibitions on any expressive activity blocking the entrance to a public building. The government has more power to impose content neutral regulations on expression, as it must only pass intermediate scrutiny, meaning the law "[1] advances important governmental interests [2] unrelated to the suppression of free speech and [3] does not burden substantially more speech than necessary to further those interests."[10] The lowest level of constitutional scrutiny—the easiest one for a law to pass—is the rational basis test. Rational basis is used to review laws that do not burden fundamental constitutional rights,[11] requiring only that the government show "[1] a rational relation to [2] some legitimate end."[12]

THE FACTS OF *FREE SPEECH COALITION, INC. V. PAXTON*

As the *Ginsberg* case suggests, for decades states have banned distribution of pornography to minors, particularly to prohibit their sale to children at brick-and-mortar stores.[13] However, Texas found this type of law to be ineffective at prohibiting minors' access to pornography online, so it enacted H.B. 1181, requiring commercial websites publishing or distributing material, if "more than one-third-of which is sexual material harmful

---

[7] Reed v. Town of Gilbert, Ariz., 576 U.S. 155, 163 (2015).
[8] McCullen v. Coakley, 573 U.S. 464, 478 (2014).
[9] Police Dep't of City of Chicago v. Mosley, 408 U.S. 92, 96 (1972).
[10] Turner Broad. Sys., Inc. v. F.C.C., 520 U.S. 180, 189 (1997).
[11] F.C.C. v. Beach Commc'ns, Inc., 508 U.S. 307, 313 (1993).
[12] United States v. Skrmetti, 145 S. Ct. 1816, 1828 (2025).
[13] *See* Free Speech Coal., Inc. v. Paxton, 145 S. Ct. 2291, 2299 (2025).

to minors," to verify the ages of visitors to their website.[14] The Texas law defines "sexual material harmful to minors" to include material that "(1) is designed to appeal to or pander to the prurient interest when taken as a whole and with respect to minors; (2) describes, displays, or depicts in a manner patently offensive with respect to minors various sex acts and portions of the human anatomy, including depictions of sexual intercourse, masturbation, sodomy, bestiality, oral copulation, flagellation, [and] excretory functions; and (3) lacks serious literary, artistic, political, or scientific value for minors."[15] This definition includes expression that is protected by the First Amendment for adults communicating with other consenting adults.

Texas's H.B. 1181 requires qualifying websites to verify that a visitor trying to access this pornographic material is at least 18 years of age by using "a commercial age verification system," including government-issued identification or "transactional data," such as records from employment or mortgages.[16] Penalties for a website that knowingly violates the law are significant: the Texas attorney general may seek injunctive relief against the website, and the attorney general may pursue a civil penalty of up to $10,000 for each day of non-compliance, as well as up to $250,000 if any minors access the prohibited material.

The Free Speech Coalition is a trade association group whose mission is "to protect the rights and freedoms of both the workers and businesses in the adult industry."[17] Along with the Free Speech Coalition, pornographic websites and an adult entertainment performer sued Texas Attorney General Ken Paxton to stop enforcement of the law. A US district court held that since the law restricted access to speech based on content, H.B. 1181 was subject to strict scrutiny, which the law failed. The district court issued a preliminary injunction against the law's enforcement. However, the US Court of Appeals for the Fifth Circuit found that the law regulated minors' access to material obscene for minors and only incidentally implicated privacy rights for adults, so it held that the law was subject merely to rational basis review. The court of appeals found the law

---

[14] *Id.* at 2299–2300.

[15] *Id.* at 2300 (internal quotations omitted).

[16] *Id.* at 2321 (Kagan, J., dissenting).

[17] "About the Free Speech Coalition," Free Speech Coalition, accessed July 25, 2025, https://www.freespeechcoalition.com/about-us.

passed the rational basis test and vacated the district court's injunction. The Free Speech Coalition appealed this decision to the Supreme Court.

Opinion of the Court

Justice Thomas wrote for a 6–3 majority upholding the Texas law. Emphasizing history and tradition, the Court explained how since at least the early 1800s, states exercised power to "prevent children from accessing speech that is obscene to children" because "[m]inors ... have long been thought to be more susceptible to the harmful effects of sexually explicit content."[18] For these reasons, the government has the power to ban minors from accessing more sexually explicit material than is the case for adults, even as a "State may not prohibit adults from accessing content that is obscene only to minors."[19] The Court noted how, due to smartphones and streaming platforms, "many adolescents can now access vast libraries of video content—both benign and obscene—at almost any time and place, with an ease that would have been unimaginable" when the Court decided its last case on the government's power to protect children from pornography online, *Ashcroft v. ACLU* (2004).[20]

The Court next determined the proper level of scrutiny to apply to H.B. 1181. Although Texas burdens adults' right to access sexually explicit material, the Court found that "adults have no First Amendment right to avoid age verification," meaning the law "has only an incidental effect on protected speech, making it subject to intermediate scrutiny."[21] This is so because the "power to verify age is a necessary component of the power to prevent children's access to content that is obscene from their perspective."[22] The Court recounted how age verification is required by Texas to obtain various items, such as alcohol, lottery tickets, tattoos, body piercings, fireworks, and driver's licenses; the Court explained that Texas requires proof of age to exercise other constitutional rights, including obtaining a handgun license, registering to vote, and marrying; and the Court recalled how the *Ginsberg* decision upheld requiring proof of age to purchase pornographic magazines. The Court found a greater need to verify age before

---

[18] *Free Speech Coal.*, 145 S. Ct. at 2303, 2304.
[19] *Id.* at 2304.
[20] *Id.* at 2306.
[21] *Id.* at 2306, 2309.
[22] *Id.* at 2306.

one accesses pornography online than in person, as "[u]nlike a store clerk, a website operator cannot look at its visitors and estimate their ages."[23] The Court cautioned that if it instead applied strict scrutiny to H.B. 1181, that would call into question any law mandating age verification, including in person.

Applying intermediate scrutiny to H.B. 1181, the Court found first that the law advances the important interest of "shielding children from sexual content," by blocking "minors from easily circumventing a prohibition on their accessing sexual content."[24] The Court ruled that the law was sufficiently tailored because age verification has been used both in person and online for a variety of services, making the mandate to be "plainly a legitimate legislative choice."[25] Even though there might be less restrictive ways of Texas accomplishing its goals (such as promoting parents' use of content-filtering software on their children's phones or requiring internet service providers to block pornographic content unless a household requests it), the Court ruled that those more speech protective approaches are not required by intermediate scrutiny.

Dissent

Justice Kagan wrote the dissent in *Free Speech Coalition, Inc. v. Paxton*, joined by Justices Sotomayor and Jackson. Kagan explained that adults have "a constitutional right to view the very same speech that a State may prohibit for children."[26] According to Kagan, since H.B. 1181 requires adults wishing to view constitutionally protected expression to verify their age, it burdens that expression by creating a chilling effect in ways that in person requirements do not: "It is not … like having to flash ID to enter a club. It is turning over information about yourself and your viewing habits—respecting speech many find repulsive—to a website operator, and then to … who knows? The operator might sell the information; the operator might be hacked or subpoenaed."[27] Kagan explained that the Texas law discriminates against adults' protected expression on the basis of content, as only certain types of sexually explicit speech online trigger the

---

[23] *Id.* at 2308.
[24] *Id.* at 2317.
[25] *Id.* at 2317.
[26] *Id.* at 2319 (Kagan, J., dissenting).
[27] *Id.* at 2321 (Kagan., dissenting) (internal citation omitted).

verification requirement. Therefore, Kagan argued that Supreme Court precedent—including cases where the government tried to restrict adults' access to dial-a-porn services, indecent content online, and sexually oriented cable channels—demands that H.B. 1181 should be reviewed by strict scrutiny, which Kagan characterized as "a highly rigorous but not fatal form of constitutional review."[28] This is true for the dissent because "[t]he First Amendment prevents making speech hard, as well as banning it outright."[29]

Using strict scrutiny, Kagan conceded that states undoubtedly have a compelling interest in protecting children from sexually explicit expression. However, as to the second requirement of the test—that Texas must use the least restrictive means to achieve that interest—Kagan wrote that she "would demand Texas show more, to ensure it is not undervaluing the interest in free expression."[30] Kagan chastised the majority for permitting Texas to "restrict[ ] adults' access to protected speech if that is not in fact necessary."[31] Similarly, Kagan questioned the majority's citation of states' age verification requirements for obtaining various items, as these products have nothing to do with exercising free speech rights.

IMPLICATIONS

As the opinions in *Free Speech Coalition* demonstrate, the level of scrutiny used to review a speech restriction can make a major difference in whether a law is upheld. In First Amendment cases, only once has a majority of the Supreme Court agreed that a law triggered strict scrutiny *and* satisfied it.[32] This has essentially meant the death knell for content discriminatory laws. The Court's use of intermediate scrutiny to review H.B. 1181 could signal that the Court majority is more willing to defer to the government on speech regulations. As described by the Court, intermediate scrutiny "is deferential but not toothless,"[33] although the Court declined to apply the even more deferential rational basis review, which Texas advocated in the case. Nevertheless, Kagan cited a host of Supreme Court precedents where content restrictions were judged by strict scrutiny, including cases where

---

[28] *Id.* at 2319, 2322–2324 (Kagan, J., dissenting).
[29] *Id.* at 2320 (Kagan., dissenting).
[30] *Id.* at 2331 (Kagan., dissenting).
[31] *Id.* at 2320 (Kagan., dissenting).
[32] *Id.* at 2310 (citing Holder v. Humanitarian Law Project, 561 U.S. 1, 27–39, (2010)).
[33] *Id.* at 2316.

the government's concern was shielding children from sexually explicit speech.

Government clearly possesses the power to ban the distribution of pornography to minors. But *Free Speech Coalition* also has implications for adult access to sexually oriented expression, especially as it relates to concerns about age verification online (including identity theft, blackmail, and doxxing), leading to a potential chilling effect on this type of expression among adults. The Texas law applies to websites in which one-third or more of the content is "sexual material harmful to minors." Could states seek to lower that fraction or more broadly define material meeting that definition, so that a larger number of websites would have to require age verification? As the opinion of the Court explained, Texas "does not require age verification on other sites, such as search engines and social-media websites, where children are likely to find sexually explicit content."[34] Legislatures might try to require that next, with age verification becoming necessary to access medical, educational, or artistic materials that relate to sex and sexuality.

Could states seek to use age verification requirements to deter adults from engaging in other types of expression, assuming they will pass intermediate scrutiny? Kagan argued that imposing a $20 tax on certain types of speech or limiting speech on subjects to certain days of the week are not outright total bans on expression, but they are burdens similar to demanding identification to gain access to a website about a topic.[35] In addition to sexually explicit expression, speech that is constitutionally protected but disfavored by many people—including hate speech, speech advocating law violation, speech containing cursing, or speech deemed misinformation—could be targeted for age verification and then judged merely by intermediate scrutiny. If, as the opinion of the Court noted, "in 2024, 95 percent of American teens had access to a smartphone, allowing many to access the internet at almost any time and place,"[36] state justifications to restrict access to this content online (including on streaming platforms and social-media websites) could be couched in terms of protecting minors.

Finally, the opinion of the Court in *Free Speech Coalition* made a point of emphasizing early American history.[37] This bears similarities to Supreme

---

[34] *Id.* at 2318.
[35] *Id.* at 2330 (Kagan., dissenting).
[36] *Id.* at 2314.
[37] *Id.* at 2303.

Court decisions over the last few years that have significantly shifted the Court's jurisprudence on the Establishment Clause, the Second Amendment, and reproductive rights, as the Court overturned laws and/or overruled long-standing precedents in those cases based on its reading of founding era history and tradition.[38] Since much of the Court's First Amendment free speech precedent is based on post–World War II decisions, a similar refocus on history back to the founding for free expression could result in the Court revisiting major precedents on matters like obscenity, defamation, incitement, true threats, offensive expression, and profanity.

---

[38] *See* Kennedy v. Bremerton Sch. Dist., 597 U.S. 507, 534 (2022) (The Court "abandoned" the *Lemon* test for the Establishment Clause for "[a]n analysis focused on original meaning and history."); New York State Rifle & Pistol Ass'n, Inc. v. Bruen, 597 U.S. 1, 39 (2022) (The Court overturned a state proper-cause requirement for concealed carry of firearms as not meeting a "text-and-history standard."); Dobbs v. Jackson Women's Health Org., 597 U.S. 215, 240 (2022) (The Court used "history and tradition" to conclude that "the Fourteenth Amendment does not protect the right to an abortion.").

CHAPTER 16

Ames v. Ohio Dept. of Youth Services: The White Man's Burden

Ion Meyn

An employee claims they were fired for being White. Should they face no more skepticism than if they were Black? Or should the White employee need to show something more if we are going to believe they were a victim of race discrimination?

Courts have struggled with these types of questions in cases involving Title VII, the federal law that prohibits workplace discrimination based on race, sex, national origin, color, or religion.[1] Courts all agree that Title VII's protected classes include those who are more privileged—for example, that White employees are protected under "race" and men are protected under "sex." Courts, however, have disagreed over what evidence more privileged members must produce to show that they were victims of discrimination. Over the last 45 years, a circuit court split had emerged. Some circuits held that a privileged member must show something more than non-privileged class members, where other circuits ruled that their burden was the same. In *Ames v. Ohio*, the Court resolved this split,

---

[1] Civil Rights Act of 1964, 42 U. S. C. §2000e–2(a)(1).

I. Meyn (✉)
University of Wisconsin Law School, Madison, WI, USA
e-mail: meyn@wisc.edu

© The Author(s), under exclusive license to Springer Nature Switzerland AG 2026
H. Schweber (ed.), *SCOTUS 2025*,
https://doi.org/10.1007/978-3-032-10231-7_16

holding that privileged and non-privileged members of a protected class share the same evidentiary burden in making out a case for discrimination.[2]

The opinion carries significant consequences. Legally, it will further incentivize more privileged members of Title VII's protected classes—those who are White, men, straight, or Christian—to bring discrimination claims. Politically, the case will be well cited in the fierce battle over the future of DEI programs.

The facts of the case are simple. Marlean Ames worked as an administrator with the Ohio Department of Youth Services. In 2019, she interviewed for a management position, which was left open for months until the Department promoted a gay woman.[3] During that interim, Ms. Ames was demoted, losing her position to a gay man. She alleged she was discriminated against for being straight.[4]

To survive summary judgment in Title VII litigation, an employee in most cases must follow the *McDonnell Douglas* burden-shifting framework and make out a prima facie case of discrimination—they must produce facts sufficient for us to presume that they were discriminated against because of their race, sex, national origin, color, or religion.[5] If the employee meets this forgiving and flexible standard, the burden shifts to the employer to show its decision was for a non-discriminatory reason.[6] But if the employee cannot satisfy their initial burden, the court dismisses the case.

Ms. Ames was able to show that, though she was qualified, a gay employee was promoted and another gay employee replaced her. Typically, these facts would give rise to the inference of unlawful discrimination, shifting the burden to the Department to articulate non-discriminatory reasons for these decisions.

---

[2] 605 U.S. __ (2025).

[3] *Brief for the United States as Amicus Curiae in Support of Vacatur*, No. 23-1039, p. 5 (2024) (Biden Amicus).

[4] Sexual orientation is protected under Title VII. *Bostock v. Clayton County*, 590 U.S. 644 (2020). As to her demotion claim, Ms. Ames also alleged discrimination based on her gender. This unsuccessful claim was not at issue in the Court's decision.

[5] *McDonell Douglas Corp. v. Green*, 411 U.S. 792 (1973); Sandra F. Sperino, *Irreconcilable: McDonnell Douglas and Summary Judgment*, 102 N.C.L. Rev. 459, 468 (2024).

[6] The employee must then produce evidence sufficient to convince a reasonable jury that the employer's explanation was pretextual. *McDonell Douglas Corp.*, *supra* note 5.

But not in Ms. Ames case. The lower courts reasoned that she faced a higher prima facie burden because she is straight. In the Sixth Circuit, Ms. Ames had to show "background circumstances that support the suspicion that the defendant is that unusual employer who discriminates against the majority."[7] She could do this in one of two ways. She could demonstrate through statistical evidence that the Department engaged in a pattern of discrimination against straight employees. Or she could show the decision-maker was a non-privileged member of the protected class; here, that the decision-maker was gay. The Department, however, was led by straight managers who were also the decision-makers in denying Ms. Ames the promotion and demoting her to a secretarial role.[8] Ms. Ames could not show these "background circumstances" and so the lower courts dismissed her case.

This was not a new requirement in the Sixth Circuit; it had been the rule there for 40 years.[9] The "background circumstances" rule was first articulated by the D.C. Circuit Court in 1981.[10] The rule had also been well established in the Seventh, Eighth, and Tenth Circuits.[11] Twenty years after all these circuit courts had adopted the requirement, the Court granted review.

Writing for a unanimous Court, Justice Ketanji Brown Jackson zeroed in on Title VII's language that an employer cannot discriminate against "any individual" who is a member of a protected group.[12] "By establishing the same protections for every 'individual'—without regard to that individual's membership in a minority or majority group—Congress, left no room for courts to impose special requirements on majority-group

---

[7] 605 U.S. __ (2025). Instead of "those in the majority" I refer to those class members that are privileged. The terms "majority" and "minority" refers to demographic representation that does not capture racism or sexism as constructed systems of power. In some antebellum states, Black persons outnumbered White persons, yet Black persons were racially oppressed. More recently, this dynamic was on stark display in apartheid South Africa.

[8] Biden Amicus, *supra* note 3, at 4 and 21.

[9] *Jasany v. United States Postal Service*, 755 F.2d 1244, 1252–53 (6th Cir. 1985).

[10] *Parker v. Baltimore & Ohio R.R.*, 652 F.2d 1012, 1017–18 (D.C. Cir. 1981).

[11] *Notari v. Denver Water Dep't*, 971 F.2d 585, 589 (10th Cir. 1992); *Mills v. Health Care Serv. Corp.*, 171 F.3d 450, 454–455 (7th Cir. 1999); *Hammer v. Ashcroft*, 383 F.3d 722, 724 (8th Cir. 2004).

[12] The Court's decision rested on a textual analysis of Title VII. In a footnote, the Court summarily mentions in dicta that the "background circumstances" requirement is "plainly at odds" with Equal Protection.

plaintiffs alone."[13] Justice Jackson cited *Griggs v. Duke Power*, which stated that a "discriminatory preference for any group, minority or majority, is precisely and only what Congress has proscribed."[14] She also relied on *McDonald v. Santa Fe Trail Transportation Co*, which stated, "Title VII prohibited racial discrimination against the [W]hite petitioners ... upon the same standards as would be applicable were they [Black]."[15]

Thus, the Court reasoned that if the text applies to *any member* of one of its protected classes, then *every member* of those classes must be subject to the same presumptions of harm. The Court did not confront any serious counterargument. Instead, the Court performed due diligence by tearing down Ohio's defense. The state argued the additional burden was somehow not an additional burden. That this defense begged ridicule was likely deliberate. Though on its face a case about sex discrimination, the decision enters the war over what constitutes racial equality, and Ohio Attorney General David Yost, who seeks to ban critical race from schools and dismantle DEI programming, perhaps sought a smoother glide path for White employees claiming race discrimination.[16]

One counterargument could be found in the reasoning of circuit courts. In 1981, the D.C. Circuit reasoned, "Membership in a socially disfavored group was the assumption on which the entire *McDonnell Douglas* analysis was predicated, for only in that context can it be stated as a general rule that the 'light of common experience' would lead a factfinder to infer discriminatory motive from the unexplained hiring of a [privileged member] rather than a [disfavored] group member."[17] The D.C. Circuit continued, "it defies common sense to suggest that the promotion of a [B]lack employee justifies an inference of prejudice against [W]hite co-workers in our present society." The Court failed to address this argument.

Interpretation of text, regardless of its source, is informed by ideology. From *Dred Scott* to *Plessy* to *Brown* to *SFFA*, the Court's assumptions

---

[13] Justice Clarence Thomas, joined by Justice Neil Gorsuch, concurred. He joined the majority opinion "in full" but addressed his general disfavor toward judge-made rules (like "background circumstances"). He also criticized the *McDonell Douglas* burden-shifting framework, while noting that the case did not present this issue.
[14] 401 U.S. 424, 431 (1971).
[15] 427 U.S. 273, 280 (1976).
[16] Laura Bischoff, *Ohio AG Dave Yost to Costco: Drop your diversity programs or else*, The Columbus Dispatch, Jan. 28, 2025; Ann Saver, *Ohio AG: Critical race theory requirements in school could violate state constitution*, The Columbus Dispatch, Sept. 14, 2021.
[17] *Parker*, 652 F.2d at 1017.

about the nature of racism have had a profound impact on case outcomes.[18] The Court has increasingly adhered to narrower conceptions of equal opportunity and formal equality.[19] This has required blinders: in the last 35 years, the Court has avoided engagement with the wealth of critical race scholarship that seeks to understand how law can construct and maintain violent systems of oppression.[20] Evident of this lack of engagement, Chief Justice John Roberts reduced racism to a colorblind platitude: "The way to stop discrimination on the basis of race is to stop discriminating on the basis of race."[21]

In *Ames*, the interpretation of Title VII's text is implicitly anchored in the assumption that different treatment is discrimination. And yet, nothing in Title VII requires that that one interpret its text through a theory of formal equality. Application of a structural understanding of discrimination potentially produces a different interpretation of the text. Under a structural view, systems of oppression are constructed with intended beneficiaries and causalities. White people construct racism. Men construct sexism. Straight people construct homophobia. Nothing in Title VII's text suggests that dissimilarly situated class members be similarly treated. Even if the employee is covered by Title VII, its text arguably does not preclude courts from exhibiting more skepticism when an intended beneficiary of racism or sexism claims they have been discriminated against because of their race or sex.[22]

Ames falls within the Court's traditional framework for resolving disputes over racial equality. And the optics—that Justice Jackson, a

---

[18] Kimberlé Crenshaw, et al., Critical Race Theory, *Introduction*, xxviii (1995).
[19] Neil Gotunda, *A Critique of "Our Constitution is Color-blind,"* 44 Stan. L. Rev. 1 (1991); Racel Moran, *The Unbearable Emptiness of Formalism: Autonomy, Equality, and the Future of Affirmative Action*, 100 N.C.L. Rev. 785 (2022).
[20] Alan David Freeman, *Legitimizing Racial Discrimination Through Antidiscrimination Law: A Critical Review of Supreme Court Doctrine*, 62 Minn. L. Rev. 1049, 1052-57 (1978); Destiny Peery, *(Re)defining Race: Addressing the Consequences of the Law's Failure to Define Race*, 38 Cardozo L. Rev. 1817, 1841-42 (2017); William M. Wiecek, *Structural Racism and the Law in America Today: An Introduction*, 100 Ky. L. J. 1 4-5 (2011/2012).
[21] *Parents Involved in Community Schools v. Seattle School District No. 1*, 551 U.S. 701, 748 (2007).
[22] Requiring more of privileged but protected claimants can be reconciled with precedent. The Court in *Griggs* held that an employee with privileged but protected traits could sue under Title VII. The Court in *McDonald* held that a privileged claimant has the right to sue under any recognized theory of liability. Neither case precludes privileged claimants from being more carefully screened.

proponent of race-conscious remedies, authored a unanimous decision on race—suggest that the case was an uncontroversial supplement to long held precedent.[23] The opinion reads as such, communicating a "nothing to see here" tone. Perhaps Justice Jackson accepted authorship to mitigate an inevitable erosion of progressive aspirations. The Left attempted to put on a good face. The Legal Defense Fund stated, "Simply put, the *Ames* decision reaffirms Title VII's antidiscrimination principles and framework ... [w]e are pleased that the Court did not use this case as an opportunity to wholly upend well-established Title VII principles and precedents."[24]

If that was the intended message, many did not get it.

Within a political moment inflamed by toxic masculinity, Replacement theory, and claims of White men being victimized, *Ames* is expected to increase the number of discrimination lawsuits brought by employees who are White, men, straight, and Christian.[25] These types of claims are on the rise and *Ames* legitimates the trend. The case also validates principles useful in arguing DEI programs discriminate against these same employees.

DEI opponents are celebrating *Ames* and the recently decided *Muldrow v. City of St. Louis*.[26] In *Muldrow*, a woman employee was gaslit under the guise of a "lateral transfer" that nonetheless reduced her prospect of advancement. The Court lowered the bar for liability and held that an employee claiming they are subject to discriminatory conditions need not show "significant harm" or "material disadvantage," but only that they were "treated worse." After conservative outlets cheered *Muldrow's* holding, the ACLU claimed its win would have no effect on DEI programming: "The fearmongering of DEI opponents has no basis in law and fundamentally misunderstands how most DEI programs work."[27]

---

[23] Michelle Travis, *Supreme Court Didn't Make DEI Illegal In* Ames *Ruling, Lawyers Explain*, Forbes, June 11, 2025.

[24] *LDF Affirms Supreme Court's Employment Discrimination Decision Leaves Civil Rights Protections Intact for Historically Marginalized Groups*, LDF, June 5, 2025.

[25] Elie Mystal, *The Supreme Court Just Cleared the Way for a Flood of "Reverse Discrimination" Lawsuits*, The Nation, June 5, 2025; Allen Smith, *SCOTUS Ruling May Increase 'Reverse Discrimination' Cases*, SHRM, June 5, 2025; Jan Wolfe and Erin Mulvaney, *Supreme Court Makes it Easier to Pursue Reverse Discrimination Claims*, Washington Post, June 5, 2025.

[26] Slip opinion, p. 6 (2024).

[27] ACLU, *Supreme Court Delivers Big Win for Workplace Equality in* Muldrow v. City *of St. Louis Ruling*, April 17, 2024.

Maybe. But *Ames* and *Muldrow* can be read to potentially legitimize claims that White men are treated worse when they must attend a DEI training that seems to blame White men for discrimination, or when a mentorship program appears to favor employees of color or women. Such lawsuits have recently found footing,[28] and with the arrival of *Ames* and *Muldrow*, law firms are urging clients to revisit DEI programs.[29] Some predict *Ames* puts DEI on uncertain ground,[30] where more bullish publications portray *Ames* as the beginning of the end for DEI.[31]

As with any legal or political movement, historical revision is at play. After all, DEI programs long preceded Title VII. Congress did not indicate that Title VII undermined these efforts. Soon after Title VII's passage, President Johnson signed Executive Order 11246, which required federal contractors to document affirmative efforts to diversify their workforce. A lawsuit that alleged this massive DEI program violated Title VII lost in the courts.[32] This history now faces revision, with President Trump ending the 60-year lifespan of Executive Order 11246 and proclaiming in a new one that "DEI" programs constitute "preferences" that "violate the text and spirit of our longstanding Federal civil-rights laws."[33]

Ames and *Muldrow* will be deployed in efforts to dismantle DEI programming embraced by Fortune 500 companies. Under the supervision of a conservative Court that recently upended 50 years of precedent to hold that race-conscious preferences in college admissions violate colorblind theory,[34] renewed efforts to cast DEI programs as a violation of Title VII will find a receptive audience. The ACLU could be forgiven for understanding *Muldrow* to increase protections for vulnerable employees. But

---

[28] Chris Marr, *Hostile Work Environment Claims Aimed at DEI Gain Early Traction*, Bloomberg Law, December 27, 2024; Nathaniel Meyersohn, *The legal war on DEI begins: Missouri sues Starbucks over its diversity programs*, CNN, February 14, 2025.

[29] See, e.g., Brian Kaplan, et al., *United States Supreme Court rejects heightened standard for "reverse discrimination" claims under Title VII*, DLA Piper, June 13, 2025.

[30] Allison Powers, et al., *Breaking—Supreme Court Unanimously Lowers Bar for "Reverse Discrimination" Claims: Ames v. Ohio Department of Youth Services Redefines Title VII Litigation*, The National Law Review, June 6, 2025.

[31] William Jacobson and James Nault, *The end is near for on-the-job reverse discrimination—another blow to DEI*, New York Post, May 18, 2025.

[32] *Contractors Assoc. of Eastern Pennsylvania v. Secretary of Labor*, 442 F.2d 159 (3d Cir. 1971).

[33] Executive Order 14173, *Ending Illegal Discrimination and Restoring Merit-Based Opportunity*, January 21, 2025.

[34] *Students for Fair Admissions v. Harvard*, 143 S.Ct. 2141 (2023).

Muldrow, and now *Ames*, are decided in the emergence of an upside-down reality, where persons of color, women, and gay persons are portrayed as beneficiaries of wokeness gone mad as White men are being excluded from workplace opportunities and advancement.

Justice Ruth Bader Ginsberg observed, "To those accustomed to privilege, equality feels like oppression." But part of privilege is being able to construct a false reality that informs the law and then is validated by that same law—a privilege reinforcing feedback loop.[35] Given the trajectory of the law, for those with privilege the emerging narratives of equal opportunity will feel less like oppression and more and more like empowerment.

---

[35] Laura E. Gómez, *Understanding Law and Race as Mutually Constitutive: An Invitation to Explore an Emerging Field*, 6 Ann. Rev. L. & Soc. Sci. 487, 488 (2021); Ian Haney Lopez, White By Law: The Legal Construction of Race (1996).

GPSR Compliance

The European Union's (EU) General Product Safety Regulation (GPSR) is a set of rules that requires consumer products to be safe and our obligations to ensure this.

If you have any concerns about our products, you can contact us on

ProductSafety@springernature.com

In case Publisher is established outside the EU, the EU authorized representative is:

Springer Nature Customer Service Center GmbH
Europaplatz 3
69115 Heidelberg, Germany

www.ingramcontent.com/pod-product-compliance
Lightning Source LLC
LaVergne TN
LVHW040146080526
838202LV00042B/3044